ANARCHY IN THE UK

THE ANGRY BRIGADE

TOM VAGUE

ENGLISH PSYCHOGEOGRAPHY SERIES

VAGUE 27 AK PRESS LONDON EDINBURGH SAN FRANCISCO 1997

A N A R C H Y   I N   T H E   U K

Previously published as 'The Boy Scout Guide to Situationism: The 20th Century and how to leave it' in Vague 16/17 Psychic Terrorism annual 1985/1989 and in part in Zigzag 1985

This revised and expanded version published by AK Press 1997

AK Press
PO Box 12766
Edinburgh
Scotland EH8 9YE

AK Press
PO Box 40682
San Francisco
California 94140-0682

Edited and designed by Tom Vague at Portobello Business Centre, 2 Acklam Road, under the Westway, London W10

Vagrants and various acknowledgements to: Andy, Boogie, Cecilia and Marcella at PBC, Barry Pateman and the Kate Sharpley Library, Carolyn Starren at Kensington Central Library and Ladbroke Grove branch, Shaun and Cherry at Calvert's, Steve Abrams, Mark Allday, Tony Allen, John Apostle, J.B, John Barker (for comments/criticisms), Sandra Belgrave, Ronan Bennett, Ian Bone, Helen Bowling, Aeneas Brown, Gordon Carr, Stuart Christie, Formerly Comic Shop Shaun, Warren C, Brian Design, Tony D, Simon Dwyer, Jon Eliot, Caroline Grimshaw, Raul Harding, Derek Harris, Perry Harris, Stewart Home, Mark Jackson, Barry Jennings, Nick Jones at the Max Jones Archive, Ramsey Kanaan, Peter Mannheim, Alexis McKay, Sean McLusky, John Mead, Mick Mercer, Simon Morrissey, Richard North, Genesis P.Orridge, Dean Plant, Dr. Dre Radosavlevich, Jez Redneck, Jamie Reid, George Robertson, Roadent, Ray Roughler-Jones, Ralph Rumney, Vermillion Sands, Jon Savage, Mark / Paul Stewart, Stokey Dave / Simon / Nick, Stringy, John Studholme, Dee Thorne, Toko, Fabian Tompsett, Camila Trajber - Ribeiro (Father Tom photo) and Liz Young

Soundtrack: Ragga in the Jungle, Sex Pistols, prag VEC, Malcolm McLaren, Billie Holiday, Juliette Greco, Miles Davis, Martha and the Vandellas, Orbital, the Who, Rolling Stones, Small Faces, David Bowie, BAD, Last Poets, Jimi Hendrix, Ry Cooder, Randy Newman, Merry Clayton Singers, Buffy Sainte-Marie, Marianne Faithfull, John Lennon, Yoko Ono, George Harrison, Jimmy Cliff, Desmond Dekker, Sly and the Family Stone, Curtis Mayfield, Isaac Hayes, Rod Stewart and the Faces, Alice Cooper, T. Rex, Mott the Hoople, Slade, Argent, Middle of the Road, New Seekers, Pink Fairies, Deviants, Hawkwind, Pink Floyd, Merle Major, MC5, New York Dolls, Culture, Mighty Diamonds, more Sex Pistols, Bay City Rollers, M, Heartbreakers, Motorhead, Peter Tosh, 101ers, Clash, Slits, Mikey Dread, Lee Perry, Dillinger, Thin Lizzy, Buzzcocks, X-Ray-Spex, Adverts, Subway Sect, Bow-wow-wow, Pop Group, ATV, TG / PTV, Crass, Joy Division, Happy Mondays, Stone Roses, Pulp, Pet Shop Boys, Pogues, NWA, Ice Cube, Cypress Hill, Intastella, Biba, Black Grape, more Jungle, Prodigy, Underworld

VAGUE 27   W111AR   1990-96   English Psychogeography Series

Printed and bound in the UK by Calvert's Press Workers Co-op   0171 - 739 - 1474

A CIP record for this title is available from the British Library and the Library of Congress

ISSN 0964 - 7023
ISBN 1 873176 98 8

'Things fall apart: The centre cannot hold: Mere anarchy is loosed upon the world.' (Yeats)

4

'Milord, I am from another country.
We are bored in the town.
There is no longer any Temple of the Sun...
The Hacienda must be built.'

'Formula for a New City', International Situationiste, 1958.

'Is this the MPLA?
Or is this the UDA?
Or is this the IRA?
I thought it was the UK,
Or just another country,
Another council tenancy.'

'Anarchy in the UK', Sex Pistols, 1976.

RETURN OF THE DURRUTI COLUMN

THE FRENCH CONNECTION - THE LETTRISTS - THE SITUATIONISTS - THE SOCIETY OF THE SPECTACLE - THE REVOLUTION OF EVERYDAY LIFE - STRASBOURG 1966 - ON THE POVERTY OF STUDENT LIFE

After the advent of Punk, the term 'Situationism' is liberally sprinkled throughout pop culture. Mostly it's attached to the activities of Malcolm McLaren and becomes synonymous with ripping off record companies. Then it passes into punk mythology as the phenomenom's hidden roots and philosophy. But the term has been around for some time before Malcolm McLaren and the Sex Pistols and has already caused quite a bit of fuss.

British police first become aware of 'Situationism' 5 years before Punk, when in 1971 the country and more specifically, the house of Robert Carr, Ted Heath's Secretary of State for Employment, is rocked by two bomb explosions. Following the attack the press receive communiques from a group calling itself 'The Angry Brigade'; *'Robert Carr got it tonight. We're getting closer.'*

To begin with all the police have on the Angry Brigade is a list of their targets; *'Embassies, High Pigs, Spectacles, Judges, Property...'* published in the underground press. But that inspires one enterprising Special Branch sergeant, the 'Situationist Cop' Roy Cremer, to start rummaging about in alternative bookshops. In due course he finds that the term 'Spectacles' is a favourite of the Paris based Situationist International. This takes the investigations away from the Tories' controversial Industrial Relations Bill and back to 1957, when the Situationists start up as an international avant-garde anti-art art group. Or something like that...

The Situationist International mostly evolves from the Lettrist International, a 40s avant-garde art group primarily concerned with being existential in Left Bank cafes such as Tabou and Mabillon and drifting round Paris for days or weeks on end, in order to create new emotional maps of the city. In the course of one such drift or dérive the Lettrist Jean-Michel Mension makes a name for himself by wearing trousers painted with slogans 25 years before Punk. The Lettrists are also prone to gatecrashing other people's gigs; making early 50s headlines by disrupting Charlie Chaplin's Paris Ritz press conference for 'Limelight'. And most notably, causing a riot when one of their number dresses as a priest and declares 'God is Dead' from the pulpit of Notre Dame.

The Lettrist Jean-Michel Mension and Fred, Boulevard St. Germain, 1950-54. Ed Van Der Elsken.

The Situationists continue the Lettrists' drifting activities and specialise in lengthy, mostly impenetrable critiques of everybody that precedes them and society in general. In their own words, from 'Internationale Situationiste' #1, June 1958, where they're at is defined thus;

CONSTRUCTED SITUATION: A moment of life concretely and deliberately constructed by the collective organization of a unitary ambiance and a game of events.

SITUATIONIST: Having to do with the theory or practical activity of constructing situations. One who engages in the construction of situations. A member of the Situationist International.

SITUATIONISM: a meaningless term improperly derived from the above. There is no such thing as situationism, which would mean a doctrine of interpretation of existing facts. The notion of situationism is obviously devised by anti-situationists.

PSYCHOGEOGRAPHY: The study of the specific effects of the geographical environment, consciously organized or not, on the emotions and behaviour of individuals.

PSYCHOGEOGRAPHICAL: Relating to psychogeography. That which manifests the geographical environment's direct emotional effects.

PSYCHOGEOGRAPHER: One who explores and reports on psychogeographical phenomena.

DERIVE: A mode of experimental behaviour linked to the conditions of urban society: a technique of transient passage through varied ambiances. Also used to designate a specific period of continuous dériving.

UNITARY URBANISM: The theory of the combined use of arts and techniques for the integral construction of a milieu in dynamic relation with experiments in behaviour.

DETOURNEMENT: Short for: détournement of pre-existing aesthetic elements. The integration of present or past artistic production into a superior construction of a milieu. In this sense there can be no situationist painting or music, but only a situationist use of these means. In a more primitive sense, détournement within the old cultural spheres is a method of propaganda, a method which testifies to the wearing out and loss of importance of those spheres.

CULTURE: The reflection and prefiguration of the possibilities of organization of everyday life in a given historical moment; a complex of aesthetics, feelings and mores through which a collectivity reacts on the life that is objectively determined by its economy. (We are defining this term only in the perspective of the creation of values, not in that of the teaching of them.)

DECOMPOSITION: The process in which the traditional cultural forms have destroyed themselves as a result of the emergence of superior means of dominating nature which enable and require superior cultural constructions. We can distinguish between an active phase of the decomposition and effective demolition of the old superstructure - which came to an end around 1930 - and a phase of repetition which has prevailed since then. The delay in the transition from decomposition to new constructions is linked to the delay in the revolutionary liquidation of capitalism.

In the early 60s, there's a purge of the more arty German and Scandinavian members, as the Situationists get political. (The Scandinavians are mostly renowned for claiming responsibility for decapitating the mermaid statue in Copenhagen harbour in 1961.) Then, after a spell with Paul Cardan's Socialisme ou Barbarie group, former Lettrist turned Situationist supremo Guy Debord comes up with his theory of the Spectacle. In his words; *'The moment when the commodity has achieved the total occupation of life.'* Debord argues that the world we see is not the real world but the 'Society of the Spectacle' (the title of his subsequent book).

According to Debord, the Spectacle is pretty much all powerful and capable of recuperating even the most radical situations, but it does have its weaknesses. Like the kind of pent-up anger and alienation unleashed in the Watts riots of 1965, and to a lesser extent the emerging hippy drop-out scene in Haight-Ashbury. Debord and the Situationists cite this sort of unconscious revolt against Spectacular Society as the first stirrings of 'the Revolution of Everyday Life'. Which is the title of the 'Society of the Spectacle' companion book by Raoul Vaneigem, in which the new Situationist manifesto is summed up thus;

To make the world a sensuous extension of man rather than have man remain an instrument of an alien world, is the goal of the Situationist revolution. For us the reconstruction of life and the rebuilding of the world are one and the same desire. To achieve this the tactics of subversion have to be extended from schools, factories, universities, to confront the Spectacle directly. Rapid transport systems, shopping centres, museums, as well as the various new forms of culture and the media, must be considered as targets, areas for scandalous activity.

Guy Debord with his missis, Michèle Bernstein (who now lives in Salisbury) and SI founding artist Asger Jorn. Paris 1961.

The Situationists first hit the headlines in 1966, when 5 'Pro-situs' or SI fans infiltrate the student union at Strasbourg University and set about scandalising the authorities. First they form an anarchist appreciation society, 'The Society for the rehabilitation of Karl Marx and Ravachol', and use union funds to produce fly-posters of Andre Bertrand's detourned 'Return of the Durruti Column' comic strip. In 'Basic Banalities' in 'IS' #8 Raoul Vaneigem sites the Spanish Civil War anarchist brigade led by Buenaventura Durruti, as the role model for the SI;

moving from town to village, liquidating the bourgeois elements and leaving the workers to see to their own self organisation.

Next the pro-situ students invite the actual Situationists to write a critique of Strasbourg University. The resulting pamphlet, 'On the Poverty of Student Life: Considered in its economic, political, sexual, and particularly intellectual aspects, and a modest proposal for its remedy' by the Tunisian Situationist Mustapha/Omar Khayati, is designed to wind up the students by confronting them with their subservience to the family and state. And it's none too subtle about it;

Every student likes to feel he is a bohemian at heart; but the student bohemian clings to his false and degraded version of individual revolt... His rent-a-crowd militancy for the latest good cause is an aspect of his real impotence... He does have marginal freedoms; a small area of liberty which as yet escapes the totalitarian control of the Spectacle: His flexible working hours permit adventure and experiment. But he is a sucker for punishment and freedom scares him to death; he feels safer in the straight-jacketed space-time of the lecture hall and the weekly essay. He is quite happy with this open prison organised for his benefit...
    The real poverty of his everyday life finds its immediate phantastic compensation in the opium of cultural commodities... He is obliged to discover modern culture as an admiring spectator... He thinks he is avant-garde if he's seen the latest Godard or 'participated' in the latest 'happening'. He discovers modernity as fast as the market can provide it: For him every rehash of ideas is a cultural revolution. His principal concern is status, and he eagerly snaps up all the paperback editions of important and 'difficult' texts with which mass culture has filled the bookstore. Unfortunately, he cannot read, so he devours them with his gaze...

Existing student rebels, such as the Dutch Provos, British 'Committee of One Hundred' and the Berkeley students, all get the thumbs down. Basically for fighting the specialised symptoms (Nuclear arms, racism, censorship) not the disease. Only the British 'Spies for Peace' get any approval from the Situationists, for releasing secret plans for a post-nuclear war government bunker in 1963. But on the other hand, away from student life, in the real world, the pamphlet points out;

13

The 'delinquents' of the world use violence to express their rejection of society and its sterile options. But their refusal is an abstract one: it gives them no chance of actually escaping the contradictions of the system. They are its products - negative, spontaneous, but none the less exploitable. All the experiments of the new social order produce them: They are the first side-effects of the new urbanism; of the disintegration of all values; of the extension of an increasingly boring consumer leisure; of the growing control of every aspect of everyday life by the psycho-humanist police force; and of the economic survival of a family unit which has lost all significance.

The 'young thug' despises work but accepts the goods. He wants what the spectacle offers him - but NOW, with no down payment. This is the essential contradiction of the delinquent's existence. He may try for a real freedom in the use of his time, in individual assertiveness, even in the construction of a kind of community. But the contradiction remains and kills. (On the fringe of society, where poverty reigns, the gang develops its own hierarchy, which can only fulfil itself in a war with other gangs, isolating each group and each individual within the group.) In the end the contradiction proves unbearable. Either the lure of the product world proves too strong, and the hooligan decides to do his honest day's work: To this end a whole sector of production is devoted specifically to his recuperation. Clothes, records, guitars, scooters, transistors, purple hearts beckon him to the land of the consumer. Or else he is forced to attack the laws of the market itself - either in the primary sense, by stealing, or by a move towards a conscious revolutionary critique of commodity society. For the delinquent only two futures are possible: revolutionary consciousness, or blind obedience on the shop floor...

We must destroy the Spectacle itself, the whole apparatus of the commodity society... We must abolish the pseudo needs and false desires which the system manufactures daily in order to preserve its power.

10,000 copies of the pamphlet are printed and handed out at the ceremony to mark the beginning of the Strasbourg academic year. An immediate outcry ensues in the local, national and international press. Including the following;

The San Francisco and London beatniks, the mods and rockers of the English beaches, the hooligans behind the Iron Curtain, all have been largely superseded by this wave of new-style nihilism. Today it is no longer a matter of outrageous hair and clothes, of dancing hysterically to induce a state of ecstacy, no longer even a matter of entering the artificial paradise of drugs. From now on, the international of young people who are 'against it' is no longer satisfied with provoking society, but intent on destroying it - on destroying the very foundations of society 'made for the rich and old' and acceding to a state of 'freedom without any kind of restriction whatsoever'.

As the pro-situ students responsible are duly expelled and the student union closed by court order, the presiding judge concludes;

"The accused have never denied the charge of misusing the funds of the student union. Indeed, they openly admit to having made the union pay for the printing of 10,000 pamphlets, not to mention the cost of other literature inspired by the 'International Situationiste'. These publications express ideas and aspirations which, to put it mildly, have nothing to do with the aims of a student union. One only has to read what the accused have written, for it is obvious that these five students, scarcely more than adolescents, lacking all experience of real life, their minds confused by ill-digested philosophical, social, political and economic theories, and perplexed by the drab monotony of their everyday life, make the empty, arrogant and pathetic claim to pass definitive judgments, sinking to outright abuse, on their fellow students, their teachers, God, religion, the clergy, the governments and political systems of the whole world. Rejecting all morality and restraint, these cynics do not hesitate to commend theft, the destruction of scholarship, the abolition of work, total subversion and a worldwide proletarian revolution with 'unlicensed pleasure' as its only goal."

- **Never Work: Preliminary Situationist programme.**
Rue de Seine, St.Germain des Prés. 1953.

15

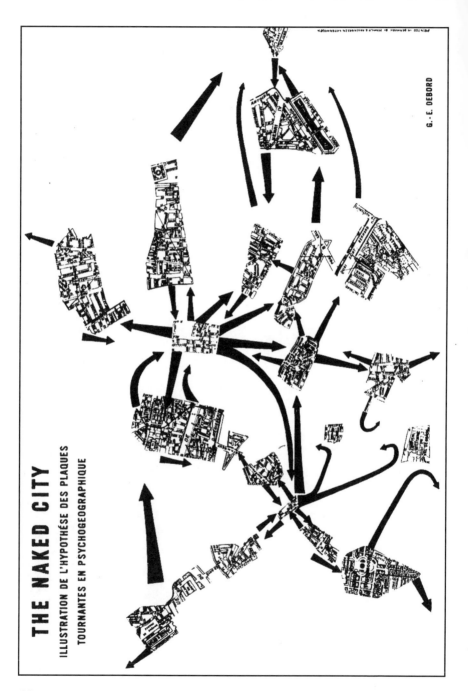

FORMULA FOR A NEW CITY

PARIS: MAY '68 - THE SORBONNE AND NANTERRE - SOCIOLOGY - PSYCHOLOGY - FUCKOLOGY - BE REALISTIC DEMAND THE IMPOSSIBLE - THE ENRAGES AND THE SITUATIONISTS IN THE OCCUPATION MOVEMENT - ON THE LEFT BANK FOR AWHILE INSANITY BOHEMIAN STYLE

'Everyone will live in their own cathedral. There will be rooms awakening more vivid fantasies than any drug. There will be houses where it will be impossible not to fall in love.'
(Ivan Chtcheglov/Gilles Ivain, 'Formulary for a New Urbanism', 1953, 'International Situationiste' #1)

The Strasbourg furore soon fizzles out, but it spreads Situationist ideas throughout the French University system, which is heading for trouble anyway, largely due to overcrowding. The government try to deal with the problem by setting up 4 new universities in the provinces and 2 off-shoots of the Sorbonne on the outskirts of Paris. But this only makes matters worse, for students and government alike. Nanterre University, to the west of Paris, becomes almost perfect for Situationist intervention. Not only is it set in particularly alienating surrounds, a far cry from the bohemian cafe scene of the Left Bank, with inadequate recreational facilities and separate sex residential blocks. It also has one of the few sociology departments in France, in which a large number of radical students are concentrated.

JANUARY 1968: After a few months of simmering discontent, a group of radical students at Nanterre draw up a list of reforms. Most of their demands are quite reasonable; like the right to specialise in subjects of their own choice; but they deliberately press on with demands they know will be rejected, as well as interrupting lectures and pelting lecturers with fruit. The students involved become known as the 'Enrages', or the 'Angry Ones'; because of their theatrical and violent nature and in honour of the original énrages, an 18th Century revolutionary group, whose leader Jacques Roux was guillotined by the Revolutionary Tribunal.

The 20th Century énrages first make the news when the Minister of Sport comes to Nanterre to open a new Olympic-swimming pool. A 'vandal orgy' is planned for the opening ceremony and the minister's route is sprayed with graffiti, but nothing happens until the minister is about to leave. Then, so the story goes, a red-haired youth steps out from the crowd and shouts;

"Minister, you've drawn up a report on French youth 600 pages long but there isn't a word in it about our sexual problems. Why not?"

The Minister replies; "I'm quite willing to discuss the matter with responsible people, but you are certainly not one of them. I myself prefer sport to sexual education. If you have sexual problems, I suggest you jump in the pool."

To which Dany Cohn-Bendit counters; "That's what the Hitler Youth used to say." And immediately shoots into the headlines and secret police files - if he's not in the latter already.

The énrages subsequently protest about police informers by parading through the hall of the Sociology building, with placards displaying blown-up pictures of police. One of the staff complains and tries to enforce the college ban on political demonstrations. There's a scuffle and the Dean calls the police. Within an hour 4 truck loads of CRS are let into the University by the Dean. The énrages shout abuse and hurl missiles, luring the police into the university so everybody can see what's going on. Then moderate students join in with the radicals and drive the police out of Nanterre.

MARCH 18: In the wake of the Tet Offensive, 3 American buildings in Paris; Chase Manhattan Bank, Bank of America and Transworld Airlines, are damaged in an anti-Vietnam war bombing campaign.

MARCH 22: After 5 members of the 'National Committee for Vietnam' are arrested for the bombings, a group of Enrages and Vietnam demonstrators occupy the administration building at Nanterre and form the 'Movement of March 22'. (From which the Enrages are almost immediately excluded over accusations of looting.)

LATE MARCH: Things develop into what the Dean describes as 'a real war psychosis', the University is closed and Cohn-Bendit and some others are summoned before a disciplinary tribunal.

APRIL: More trouble in Paris following the attempted assassination of West German student leader Rudi Dutschke.

MAY 3: Hundreds of left-wing students gather at the Sorbonne, the originally overcrowded university in Paris. The Rector of the University, Paul Roche, becomes worried, especially when he hears that a group of right-wing students are gathering nearby. He calls the Minister of Education and they decide to bring in the police, despite what happened at Nanterre. The CRS arrive and start bundling groups of students into trucks. As the first load is being driven away, the crowd start jeering and a stone is thrown through the windscreen of the truck hitting one of the police. Then the

Angry 1968 : Paris students protest

students surge forward to try and free their friends. Tear gas is fired and the violence escalates: CRS beating innocent by-standers and street fighters alike. The students setting light to cars and tearing up paving stones to hurl at the police.

The rioting spreads throughout the Latin Quarter and at the end of the first day nearly 600 people have been arrested and hundreds more injured. The students proceed to hold their ground for a week; with, each day, more and more young people joining the increasingly violent demonstrations. The authorities' heavy handling of the situation provides thousands of young Parisians with something concrete to release their pent-up anger and alienation on.

MAY 6: 20,000 students march from Denfert Rochereau to St. Germain des Prés calling for the release of those arrested over the weekend. Up to 450 more arrests and 800 woundings ensue.

MAY 7: The student union (UNEF) and teaching union (SNESup) call a strike and demand the withdrawal of the police from the Latin Quarter, the release of those arrested and the reopening of closed university faculties. Then 50,000 students and teachers march to the Arc de Triomphe behind a banner declaring 'Vive La Commune', singing the 'Internationale'.

MAY 10: The 'Night of the Barricades' on rue Gay Lussac, as the students set about occupying the whole of the Latin Quarter. The CRS eventually manage to clear rue Gay-Lussac but the writing is on the wall, literally and metaphorically.

MAY 11: Pompidou finally withdraws the CRS from the Latin Quarter and says the case of the arrested students will be reconsidered and the university reopened. But things have gone too far for this to make much difference. As news of the Events spreads, via TV-footage of street fighting and burning barricades, thousands of young people from, not just France but, all over Europe make for Paris.

Amongst the English contingent are Chris Bott, the anarchist Michael Caine, and Anna Mendelson, who will put the ideas they experience into practice back home and go down in history, as well as literally in Anna Mendelson's case, as part of 'The Angry Brigade.' Also, if you believe the story, Malcolm McLaren is given a guided tour of the barricades by his art school buddy Fred Vermorel and returns to put the ideas into practice in another way. In the Solidarity group pamphlet, another English student describes the experience thus;

The first impression was of a gigantic lid suddenly lifted, of pent-up thoughts and aspirations suddenly exploding, on being released from the realm of dreams into the realm of the real and the possible. In changing their environment people themselves were changed. Those who had never dared say anything before suddenly felt their thoughts to be the most important thing in the world and said so. The shy became communicative. The helpless and isolated suddenly discovered that collective power lay in their hands. The traditionally apathetic suddenly realised the intensity of their involvement. A tremendous surge of community and cohesion gripped those who had previously seen themselves as isolated and impotent puppets, dominated by institutions that they could neither control nor understand. People just went up and talked to one another without a trace of self-consciousness. This state of euphoria lasted throughout the whole fortnight I was there.

The most obvious sign of this new freedom of expression is the graffiti and fly-posters that suddenly appear everywhere, inspiring both communique writers and t-shirt designers alike;

'BE REALISTIC DEMAND THE IMPOSSIBLE', 'TAKE YOUR DESIRES FOR REALITY', 'IT IS FORBIDDEN TO FORBID', 'CULTURE IS THE INVERSION OF LIFE', 'SCREAM, STEAL, EJACULATE YOUR DESIRES', 'THE MORE YOU CONSUME THE LESS YOU LIVE', 'THEY ARE BUYING YOUR HAPPINESS, STEAL IT', 'GO AND DIE IN NAPLES WITH CLUB MEDITERRANEE', 'ART IS DEAD DO NOT CONSUME ITS CORPSE', 'IF GOD EXISTED WE WOULD HAVE TO SUPPRESS HIM', 'RUN FORWARD COMRADE, THE OLD WORLD IS BEHIND YOU.'
(Incidentally back in the UK Louis Armstrong's 'Wonderful World' is No.1.)

MAY 13: In spite of the CRS withdrawal, the CGT and all the main trade unions come out on strike in sympathy with the students. Paris is subsequently brought to a standstill by a massive march from Place de la Republique, through the Latin Quarter to Place Denfert Rochereau. After the CRS withdraw from the Sorbonne the students move in, replacing all the tricoleres with red and black flags and filling all the lecture halls for continuous debating sessions.

MAY 14: Euphoric celebrations at the Sorbonne Assemblee Generale as news comes through of the first factory occupation (of the Sud Aviation plant at Nantes).

MAY 16: Workers occupy the Renault plants at Cleon, near Rouen, and Flins, followed by factories all over France, culminating with the massive Boulogne Billancourt Renault plant in Paris.

MAY 17: As students march in solidarity with the Renault workers from the Sorbonne to Boulogne Billancourt, the Enrages and Situationists, who've taken over the Centre Censier, send a telegram to China;

```
* MAY 17 1968 / POLITBUREAU OF THE CHINESE COMMUNIST
PARTY GATE OF CELESTIAL PEACE PEKING SHAKE IN YOUR
SHOES BUREAUCRATS . THE INTERNATIONAL POWER OF THE
WORKERS COUNCILS WILL SOON WIPE YOU OUT . HUMANITY WILL
, ONLY BE HAPPY THE DAY THAT THE LAST BUREAUCRAT IS
STRUNG UP BY THE GUTS OF THE LAST CAPITALIST . LONG
LIVE THE FACTORY OCCUPATIONS. LONG LIVE THE GREAT
PROLETARIAN CHINESE REVOLUTION OF 1927 BETRAYED
BY THE STALINISTS. LONG LIVE THE PROLETARIAT OF CANTON
AND ELSEWHERE WHO TOOK UP ARMS AGAINST THE SO-CALLED
POPULAR ARMY . LONG LIVE THE WORKERS AND STUDENTS OF
CHINA WHO ATTACKED THE SO-CALLED CULTURAL REVOLUTION
AND THE BUREAUCRATIC MAOIST ORDER . LONG LIVE
REVOLUTIONARY MARXISM . DOWN WITH THE STATE .
* OCCUPATION COMMITTEE OF THE AUTONOMOUS AND POPULAR SORBONNE
```

MAY 18: General de Gaulle cuts short a state visit to Romania, as the strikes and occupations spread throughout France.

MAY 21: By now 9 million French workers are on strike, most factories are occupied, the French transport system has come to a standstill, and everybody from pro-footballers to film directors are supporting the students. At the Centre Censier, the Enrages and Situationists (namely Debord, Khayati, Vaneigem and the two Renés, Reisel and Vienét) form the 'Council for the Maintenance of the Occupations' and put out endless leaflets advocating a network of worker/student action-committees (a la Socialisme ou Barbarie). Whilst, at the same time,

denouncing the Communist Party and the CGT, for turning the students' revolution into a trade union demand for a pay rise. 'Red Dany' Cohn-Bendit ends up calling them 'Stalinist Scum'.

MAY 28: De Gaulle makes a secret flight to Baden-Baden in West Germany, where General Massu, the Commander of the French troops, is stationed on NATO exercises. Tanks are reported on the outskirts of Paris.

MAY 29: As Man United beat Benfica 4-1 in the '68 European Cup Final at Wembley, De Gaulle returns to Paris with Massu's assurance that the army will support him in any confrontation. Then he calls Pompidou and the Cabinet to tell them he's going to dissolve the National Assembly and call an election.

MAY 30: 4.30pm: De Gaulle addresses the Nation and basically lies that France is threatened by a 'communist dictatorship' and that, if necessary, he will have no hesitation in calling in General Massu and his troops.

And that's it. The old communist bogeyman is enough to whip up enough patriotic fervour to get the Centre to join with the Right and recuperate the situation. Extra petrol rations and free coaches are laid on and they come from all over France to Place de la Concorde, for a carefully orchestrated march to the Eternal Flame at the Arc de Triomphe. In early June the Metro starts running again, the Renault workers are evicted and the CRS successfully enforce a ban on any further demonstrations. In the elections that follow De Gaulle is returned to power by the biggest majority in recent French history... Well and truly recuperated.

Despite the millions on strike and the thousands on the streets, 'the Movement' is basically an intellectual thing. At the end of the day the workers can't relate to the intellectual repression felt by the students. Though there are certainly times throughout May when class barriers come down. De Gaulle is lucky, it's a close run thing. The students succeed in bringing out the discontent in French society, if not the World, as well as consigning old guard trad left communism to the dustbin of history. And for a month at least, everything is really up for grabs... Or is it all a CIA plot? In 1974 the American 'New Solidarity' paper of the 'National Caucus of Labour Committees' reports;

The Makhnist Situationist International pig countergang created by the CIA from scratch in 1957 in France under the slogans 'Kill the Vanguards!', 'Workers Councils Now!', and 'Create Situations!' is the paradigm example of a CIA synthetic all-purpose formation. The loose and programless anarchist 'left cover' countergang of the SI model is ideal for the CIA for the recruitment of new agents, the launching of psywar operations, the detonation of riots, syndicalist workers' actions, student power revolts, etc, the continual generation of new countergang formations, and infiltration, penetration and dissolution of socialist and other workers' organizations... During the 1968 French general strike the Situationists united with Daniel Cohn-Bendit and his anarchist thugs in preventing any potential vanguard from assuming leadership of the strike - thus guaranteeing its defeat.

Whatever it is, it takes several months before Spectacular Society is fully restored: State property has to be reclaimed, graffiti and flyposters removed and foreign students deported; including Dany Cohn-Bendit. But, with France back in the grip of a right-wing, nationalistic fervour, the show is over. Nothing much happens in Paris until Carlos the Jackal hits town in the mid 70s. After May '68, the Situationist International becomes famous, but goes downhill in a series of expulsions, resignations and scissions until it's eventual demise in 1972. Situationist ideas and influences re-emerge sporadically in America and in West Germany, through the former Situationist Dieter Kunzelmann's Kommune 1, who influence the Baader-Meinhof group. But from this point on the Situationist influence and the Anarchist action mostly moves with the English students back to the UK.

Situationist cartoon strip found flyposted outside 'International Times' office in Covent Garden and subsequently reproduced on the cover of 'it' #26, Spring 1968.

THE KIM PHILBY DINING CLUB

1968 - 1971: ABSOLUTE BEGINNERS - POWIS SQUARE - GROSVENOR SQUARE - SPANISH BOMBS - THE FIRST OF MAY GROUP - PAINT IT BLACK - PLAY WITH FIRE - DEAR BOSS - THE WILD BUNCH - MISS WORLD

'Paris '68 was rich in nameless wildness, but it was marred by a small group of embittered scene-creamers, who called themselves Situationists, and who tried in typically French fashion to intellectualize the whole mood out of existence, and with their very name tried to colonize it. Failed activists and mini-Mansonettes who boasted that all their books and pamphlets ('Leaving the 20th Century', 'The Veritable Split in the Fourth International', etc) had been produced from the proceeds of a bank robbery when even the most lavish of them could have been produced for the price of a few tins of cat-food from Safeways (one tiny exception being 'Ten Days that Shook the University' by Omar Khayati)... Their heroes are a legion of mad bombers: Ravachol, Valerie Solanas, Nechayev, the IRA, et al.'
(Heathcote Williams, 'International Times', 1977.)

There's been some Situationist influence in the UK since the 50s, but until May '68 it remains an obscure cult thing. Mostly the influence comes from Alex Trocchi, the Scottish/Italian beatnik author of 'Cain's Book' and 'Young Adam', and the quasi-situ (proto-Internet) Project Sigma. Trocchi is an early SI member and something of a situ-cause celebre, as he's always being busted for drugs. His mates include Michael X and William Burroughs and the London underground press scene (pretty much) comes out of the book/record shop, which he runs with UFO club founder John Hopkins on Powis Square in Notting Hill. Which is of course London's answer to Watts, Haight Ashbury and the Latin Quarter.

25

Before Trocchi the artist Ralph Rumney is a founder member and one of the first expulsions (for failing to hand in a psychogeographic report on Venice on time). In 1960 the 4th SI conference is held in London (at the 'British Sailors Society' in Whitechapel and the ICA in Dover Street) and by the mid-60s there's an actual English section of the SI, who publish their own magazine 'Heatwave'. During the LSE occupation in February 1967 Strasbourg pamphlets are distributed and Vaneigem's 'Revolution of Everyday Life' and 'Totality for Kids' are the first situ texts translated into English. In 'Underground (London Alternative Press 1966-74)', Nigel Fountain describes the situationist appeal to the UK hippy scene thus;

Now they were seeping into the consciousness of people within a milieu which, rejecting straight left politics, was searching for a route out of a hippy enclave at a time when the political temperature was rising... It was an appealing image, and an appealing movement for radicals hunting their red snark, and tired of waiting for Godot. It promised involvement, rationalized non-organization, it dramatized outcast status, and offered the possibility of action, and, as the next decade opened, provided it for a few...

SUMMER 1968: Cambridge and Essex universities become England's answer to the Sorbonne and Nanterre for hotbeds of radical student activity. Though typically for England the most famous Paris-style occupations are at art colleges. Most notably, Hornsey and Guildford. Malcolm McLaren does his bit at Croydon Art School, organising a sit-in with future Pistols artist Jamie Reid and Robin Scott (who also goes onto 'Pop Music' fame with 'M').

OCTOBER: Cambridge gets it's own pro-situ group, with the formation of the 'Kim Philby Dining Club', who produce a Strasbourg-style pamphlet.

OCTOBER 27: Radical students attempt to emulate the May events in Paris, by diverting a massive anti-Vietnam war march into Grosvenor Square to lay siege to the American Embassy. But it doesn't come to much. The police lines hold and afterwards demonstrators and police link arms to sing 'Auld Lang Seine', as skinheads chant 'Students, Students, Ha ha ha!' Down and out in Paris and London. While in West Germany Baader/Ensslin are jailed for arson and worldwide the Palestinians are getting into hijacking.

FEBRUARY 3, 1969: Unexploded bombs found at the Bank of Spain and the Bank of Bilbao in London.

FEBRUARY 9: A bomb goes off at the Liverpool Bank of Spain.

MARCH 15: Another bomb goes off at the London Bank of Bilbao and two anarchists, Alan Barlow and Phil Carver are arrested. A communique is found in their possession claiming responsibility for the 'International First of May Group';

Sirs, the imprisonments, deportations, and murders suffered by the people of Spain since their subjection in the Civil War, the garrotted, and those who died by the hand of Francisco Franco oblige us to respond. The blood of our brothers is as precious to us as the money and the property belonging to Spanish capitalists and their Wall Street colleagues. Let them hear this week another noise other than the clink of bloodied silver. Cease the repression. If not expect more widespread reprisals. The International 1st of May Group.

1st of May / The International Revolutionary Solidarity Movement come out of the CNT Spanish anarchist scene and has been active in England for some time. After the capture and execution of Francisco Sabate in 1960, Spanish anarchism becomes a more clandestine international affair, mostly based in Brussels. 1st of May start up on May 1 1966 with the kidnapping of a Spanish Embassy official at the Vatican. The following year their spokesman, Octavio Alberola (an old co-hort of Castro and Che Guevara) announces the failure of 'Operation Durruti'; an attempt to kidnap the US Commander-in-Chief in Spain; and the continuation of 1st of May's international activities. 1st of May arrive on the English scene on August 20 1967, with a drive-by machine-gun attack on the American Embassy in Grosvenor Square. The accompanying communique reads;

Stop criminal murders of the American Army. Solidarity with all people battling against Yankee fascism all over the world. Racism no. Freedom for American Negroes. Revolutionary Solidarity Movement.

In 1968, their pan-european bombing campaign (in support of various Latin American guerrilla groups) includes attacks on the Spanish Embassy in Belgrave Square and the American Officer's Club at Lancaster Gate. (1st of May graffiti can still be seen to this day by the Spanish School on Portobello Road.)

JUNE: After tearing up his final exam papers, John Barker drops out of university and returns to London, with fellow Cambridge pro-situ Jim Greenfield. For awhile the two stay at Barker's parents place in Willesden. Barker's father is a journalist, whilst Greenfield, who was in the same college as Prince Charles, is the son of a lorry driver from Widnes. After working on a building site in Berkhamsted for a bit they end up running a second-hand bookstall in Queen's Crescent market, Camden. Barker also helps out at the Camden High Road poster workshop, where he gets to know Paris veteran Chris Bott, who's gravitating towards the Socialisme ou Barbarie / SI influenced Solidarity group. (Not to be confused with the International Revolutionary Solidarity Movement or New Solidarity. If there's one thing worse than the International Revolutionary Solidarity Movement it's New Solidarity.)

JULY 5: The Stones play Hyde Park after the death of Brian Jones and Malcolm McLaren organises a festival/mini-riot at Goldsmith's College of Art.

JULY 18: Middle East terrorism comes to London with PFLP firebomb attack on Marks and Spencer's.

AUGUST 16: The home of far-right Tory MP Duncan Sandys is firebombed.

AUGUST 17: The Ulster Office in Saville Row gets the same treatment during Irish civil rights demo, following Londonderry riots and subsequent deployment of British troops in Northern Ireland.

AUGUST 19: A bomb is thrown into an army recruiting office in Brighton.

LATE AUGUST: Bob Dylan Isle of Wight festival.

SEPTEMBER 3: 144 Piccadilly, next to the Hilton is squatted by the London Arts/Street Commune, assorted pro-situs and hells angels.

OCTOBER 12: The 'it' office on Endell Street is occupied by a disillusioned underground faction backed up by hells angels.

NOVEMBER: Anti-Vietnam war firebomb attacks on US targets in West Berlin, as Baader/Ensslin go underground.

JANUARY 1970: Still in search of a more bohemian atmosphere, John Barker inevitably ends up 'out on the Left', sharing a flat with Mike Sirros, a Greek with FLQ (French Canadian Separatist) connections at 25 Powis Square. Which, believe it or not, is the house Donald Cammell and Nic Roeg use in May '68 for 'Turner's House' in 'Performance'. (Whether or not the vibes between Mick Jagger and James Fox effect Barker is open to debate. But is that a cool coincidence or what?) Barker becomes involved in the Notting Hill People's Association, which comes out of the London Free School scene, whose centre is just up the road at 90 Talbot Road. There he hangs out with Chris Allen, Jerry Osner and Sarah Poulikakou, who live at 89 Talbot Road, and involves himself with such community activism as outbidding property speculators and building floats for the Notting Hill Carnival. Barker is also a founder member of the West London Claimants Union, whose manifesto declares;

Our movement must challenge the whole nature and purpose of 'work' in this society. We mustn't batter on the doors of the present system for re-admittance to the treadmill of wage slavery. Wages are the expression of the price of labour as a commodity, like nuts and bolts, and not as real living human beings. We want an adequate income for all without condition. A welfare system should feed, clothe, and provide for all its citizens as of right. The present system fails to do this. Every Claimant's daily existence is a maddening struggle against poverty, under-nourishment, depression, boredom, despondency and anxiety. We want more than just a rise in the benefit scales. We demand a minimum income per person (every single member of the population) with no strings attached.

John Barker. Hey, dig the time is right for violent revolution.

Meanwhile, Jim Greenfield meets up with Anna Mendelson and Hilary Creek, two fellow university drop-outs from Essex, and gets involved in the North London squatting/commune scene around Stamford Hill and Hackney. In 'The Angry Brigade: The Cause And The Case' by Gordon Carr, a lot is made of the real politics of community action preparing Barker, Creek, Greenfield and Mendelson for 'an all out attack on society itself.' Incidentally 'Two Little Boys' by Rolf Harris is at No. 1.

FEBRUARY 10: Ian Purdie, a longstanding political activist, gets 9 months for petrol-bombing the Saville Row Ulster Office.

FEBRUARY 20: 3 students from Essex University are arrested for an attempted firebomb attack on Barclays Bank, in protest at Barclays' South African connections. John Lennon's 'Instant Karma' enters the charts.

LATE FEBRUARY: Barker and Greenfield attend a meeting at Freedom Press in Whitechapel High Street, organised by 'The International Black Cross'. This group has been revived by Stuart Christie, who is already renowned for attempting to assassinate Franco in 1964 and spending 3 years (of a 21 year sentence) in Spanish jails as a result. The main speaker is Miguel Garcia, a Spanish anarchist from the Civil War, who has resided for 20 years in the same establishments as Christie. In 'The Christie File', the first meeting of the author and John Barker is described thus;

(Barker) agreed that the anarchist Black Cross was the only viable organ in Britain which interpreted anarchism as he understood it. For semantic reasons he and his friends preferred to avoid describing themselves as anarchists and chose the more vague libertarian socialist. We obviously had a lot in common. We didn't know how important our meeting was to the spider's web being cast around us.

According to Gordon Carr, the Freedom Press meeting is a pivotal event in the formation of the ideas that become the Angry Brigade. You take some English disillusionment, add some French Situationism, and explosives, then some Spanish Anarchism, and BANG! You've got Anarchy in the UK. (There's also an American influence of course from the Weathermen and Black Panthers.) Shortly after the meeting, so this theory goes, a deal is struck between 1st of May and the embryonic Angry Brigade. In the BBC Angry Brigade documentary (also by Gordon Carr), some other 'vague libertarian socialists', including Chris Allen and Ian Purdie, discuss their thinking at the time;

"The Ruling Class just defines violence in terms of a violent picket, or a violent crime, or a violent bank robbery, or a violent bomb going off, which totally distorts the real essence of what violence is. What violence is, is the fact that people end up so freaked about the way they live, that they beat up the people they love. What people wanted to do was to try to show that that level of violence should be channelled towards the people who are actually creating the situation of oppression in the first place."

"It's a message passed onto the ruling class. OK your conspiracy will continue and the bombs won't make that much difference to the way it operates. But it's going to be just a little bit more difficult for you. We're not just going to sit around and produce petitions against what you're doing. The bombings are not going to be the be-all and end-all of the situation. They're an announcement of a certain situation where we're no longer going to accept the confines of legality set by the state."

MAY: As Everton become league champions, 'Oz' #28 the 'Schoolkids' issue comes out and the 3 Essex students are found guilty of attempted arson.
MAY 4: The American Embassy in Grosvenor Square, ever the popular target, is firebombed. This time in response to Kent State National Guard student killings.
MAY 10: After a phone warning an unexploded bomb is discovered on an Iberian airliner at Heathrow. Similar devices are found at other European airports on other Iberia planes.
MAY 14: Ulrike Meinhof assists in the springing of Andreas Baader from prison in West Berlin.
MAY 22: Another unexploded bomb is found on the site of the new Paddington

Green Police station on the Harrow Road. Home Office forensics expert Donald Lidstone subsequently finds similarities between the Heathrow and Paddington bombs. Paddington gets no publicity at the time but becomes known as the first Angry Brigade bomb attack.

JUNE 8: Just before Ted Heath's Conservatives take over from Harold Wilson's Labour administration, the 'Oz' offices on Princedale Road are busted for the 'Schoolkids' issue.

JUNE 10: Brixton Conservative Association is firebombed.

JUNE 11: Police raid the home of Stuart Christie with an explosives warrant. Christie had also been suspected of an attempted rocket attack on the Greek Embassy in 1968. 'Yellow River' by Christie at No. 1. Straight up.

LATE JUNE: The UK's Summer of Festivals begins with the first Glastonbury.

JUNE 30: Ian Purdie is released from Albany prison, after doing 9 months for the Ulster Office petrol-bombing. Meanwhile in London, there's another fire-bomb attack on the Kimber Road Army depot in Southfields.

JULY 3: Simultaneous bomb attacks on Spanish tourist offices in London and Paris, and various Spanish and Greek embassies. Also more fire-bomb attacks on Army recruiting centres in Holborn and South London.

JULY 24-26: Most hippies are out of town at Worthing Phun City.

AUGUST 9: A demo about persistent police raids on the Mangrove West Indian restaurant on All Saints Road (just round the corner from Powis Square) results in the arrest and protracted trial of the 'Mangrove 9'. (Mangrove owner Frank Critchlow's previous venture, the Rio on Westbourne Park Road had been frequented by Christine Keeler and Stephen Ward and played its part in the Profumo affair.) Meanwhile 'it' pop cult guru Mick Farren (also of Deviants fame) launches the UK branch of the White Panthers at the Jimi Hendrix Isle of Wight festival.

AUGUST 18: 3 months after the unexploded bombs at Heathrow and Paddington, a bomb goes off in the Iberia Airlines Office on ‐Regent Street.

AUGUST 30: Another bomb explodes at the Roehampton home of Metropolitan Police Commissioner Sir John Waldron. This one is accompanied by the first Angry Brigade communique; in the style of London's most famous terrorist Jack the Ripper.

DEAR BOSS
.. .YOU HAVE BEEN SENTENCED
TO DEATH BY THE REVOLUTIONARY.
TRIBUNAL FOR CRIMES OF OPPRESSION
AGAINST MANY WHO ARE OPPOSED TO
THE CAPITALIST REGEIME WHICH YOU
KEEP IN POWER.
   THE EXECUTIONER HAS BEEN SEVEERLY
REPRIMANDED FOR FAILING. NE WILL
MAKE NO FURTHER .MISTAKES.
    BUTCH CASSIDY
    THE SUNDANCE KID P.P.THE TRIBUNAL

At this stage the best motive Special Branch can come up with is resentment over the 'Garden House Affair': During a demo against the Greek Colonels' regime, earlier in the year, some Cambridge students break into a hotel hosting a 'Greek Week' dinner and brandish chairs at guests. 6 of the students arrested had just received 6 to 18 month prison sentences, causing fairly widespread outrage.

SEPTEMBER 8: This possibility gains further credence with the bombing of the Chelsea home of Attorney-General Sir Peter Rawlinson; which is accompanied by a similar communique.

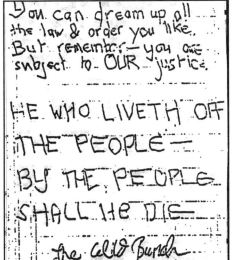

SEPTEMBER 17: Jake Prescott, a (cell) mate of Ulster Office bomber Ian Purdie, is released from Albany on parole. He heads for Notting Hill and becomes involved in the scene around Powis Square.

SEPTEMBER 18: Jimi Hendrix chokes to death on his own vomit at the Samarkand, across Ladbroke Grove on Lansdowne Crescent. One thing that Jake Prescott doesn't get accused of.

SEPTEMBER 21: Wimbledon Conservative Association is fire-bombed.

SEPTEMBER 26: In the wake of the PFLP Leila Khaled triple-hijacking and subsequent British capitulation, there are more bomb attacks aimed at Iberia Airlines around Europe. This time 1st of May succeed in blowing up a lounge used by Iberia Airlines at Heathrow. Same day the Hampstead Conservative Association is firebombed and 'Paranoid' by Black Sabbath enters the charts. While in West Germany the Red Army Faction are robbing banks.

OCTOBER 7: Booby trapped grenade found at BOAC Air terminal at Victoria.

OCTOBER 8: Another bomb goes off at the Attorney General's home because the first one hasn't been reported. The Press Association hasn't been reporting the incidents, in case the idea of urban guerrilla war in mainland Britain catches on.

OCTOBER 9: The Italian Job: A series of bombs go off simultaneously at Italian targets around Europe. Including the Italian Trade Centre in Cork Street, London and the Italian Consulates in Birmingham and Manchester. The attacks are to publicise the death of the anarchist, Giuseppe Pinelli in 1969. Pinelli supposedly threw himself out of a 4th floor Milan police station window during interrogation. The accompanying communiques proclaim; *'The manner of my death cannot be concealed. Lotta Continua!'* The Pinelli connection makes Stuart Christie, who's known to have been in contact with him, prime suspect in the eyes of Special Branch. Christie also lives in the same house as the Bank of Bilbao bombers and his job is converting appliances for North Sea gas. As Gordon Carr points out, the unexploded bombs consist of batteries and lighter-heads used to ignite North Sea gas appliances. So Christie now comes in for round-the-clock surveillance, and 'almost respectable' Fleet Street anarchist, Albert Meltzer (who publishes 'Black Flag' and 'Floodgates of Anarchy' with Christie) is asked by Special Branch to calm things down.

OCTOBER 24: During the Council workers' strike a bomb explodes in the cleaning department head office at Greenford.

OCTOBER 26: The Administration building at Keele University and Barclays Bank in Stoke Newington are firebombed.

NOVEMBER: Jim Greenfield gets nicked in Wivenhoe, Essex for stealing 2 turkeys, and subsequently gets a fine.

NOVEMBER 5: The arrest of the Powis Square 8 at a bonfire party/squat of the closed off Powis Square. As 'Performance' finally comes out and Michael X is committed for trial over the 'Slave Collar' affair at his 'Black House'.

NOVEMBER 7: A group of hippies invade the stage during the David Frost Show on LWT featuring Yippie leader Jerry Rubin (fresh from the Chicago 8 trial). The 'Frost Freakout' as it becomes known, is the Bill Grundy interview of the hippy era. Rubin and co are subsequently deported. Same day 'Voodoo Chile' by Jimi Hendrix is re-released. Also in the news; Beatles splitting up, football hooliganism, power strike and rioting in Northern Ireland as Bernadette Devlin is jailed.

NOVEMBER 20: 2.30am: A BBC Outside Broadcast van is blown up outside the Albert Hall, where later in the day the 'Miss World Contest' is due to take place. Shortly after the explosion, a group of youths are seen running away down Kensington Gore towards Notting Hill. The bombing doesn't effect the contest itself, but a 'Carry on Girls' style flour/smoke-bombing by Women's Lib does; for awhile at least. In due course some order is restored to proceedings and Bob Hope poignantly announces; "These things can't go on much longer. They're going to have to get paid off sooner or later. Someone upstairs will see to that. Anybody who wants to interrupt something as beautiful as this must be on some kind of dope."

The women are duly arrested and the show goes on as planned. But the 'Miss World' bombings do at least get some publicity; unlike the next effort...

DECEMBER 3: Late at night, a car speeds past the Spanish Embassy in Belgrave Square and a machine gun opens up. This attempt to emulate the 1967 US Embassy attack is a protest against the sentencing to death of Basque nationalists, the Burgos 6. However, only one bullet hits the Embassy. It makes a hole in a window and drops down behind a curtain, where a cleaning lady discovers it 2 days later. In the end ETA have to kidnap a West German honorary consul in order to get the death sentences lifted.

DECEMBER 5: In an attempt to overcome the press blackout, the first proper 'Angry Brigade Communique' is delivered to 'International Times'. To authenticate it and future communiques a stamp is made up from a child's 'John Bull' printing set. The name 'Angry Brigade' is chosen as a combination of the French 'Enrages' and the Spanish Anarchist Brigades, with a passing nod to the English Angry Young Men of the 50s;

BROTHERS AND SISTERS: We expect the news of the machine-gunning of the Spanish Embassy in London on Thursday night to be suppressed by the bourgeois press... It's the third time over the last month that the system has dropped the mask of the so-called 'freedom of information' and tried to hide the fact of its vulnerability... 'They' know the truth behind the BBC the day before the Miss World farce; 'they' know the truth behind the destruction of property of High Court judges; 'they' know the truth behind the four Barclays Banks which were either burned or badly destroyed; 'they' also know that active opposition to their system is spreading. The Angry Brigade doesn't claim responsibility for everything. We can make ourselves heard in one way or another. We machine-gunned the Spanish Embassy last night in solidarity with our Basque brothers and sisters. We were careful not to hit the pigs guarding the building as representatives of British capital in fascist Spain. If Britain co-operates with France over this 'legal' lynching by shutting the truth away, we will take more careful aim next time. SOLIDARITY & REVOLUTION. LOVE. COMMUNIQUE. THE ANGRY BRIGADE.

That same week another communique-cum-footnote is delivered to 'International Times';

Fascism and oppression will be smashed - Embassies (Spanish Embassy machine-gunned Thursday), High Pigs, Spectacles, Judges, Property... COMMUNIQUE 1. THE ANGRY BRIGADE.

DECEMBER 9: Following big demonstrations against the Tories' Industrial

Relations Bill, there's another bombing. This time it's the Department of Employment and Productivity in St. James's Square. After two calls to the press, police search the building just before the bomb goes off in the basement.

Success. Min. E. & Prod. COMMUNIQUE 2. THE ANGRY BRIGADE.

The next communique, which appears in 'it' #94 and 95, goes into more detail describing the DEP bombing as;

...part of a planned series of attacks on capitalism and government property... We will answer their force with our class violence. COMMUNIQUE 3. THE ANGRY BRIGADE.

MID-DECEMBER: John Barker, who's now hitched up with Hilary Creek, quits Powis Square (because he's fed up with all the do-gooding social workers in the area) and moves to Manchester. There the two buy a slum house for £400 in Cannock Street, Moss Side and turn it into a commune. Amongst the Cannock Street commune's many visitors are Ian Purdie and Jake Prescott. Purdie is described as another pro-situ Kim Philby fan, who once writes from prison;

To me Philby is the real life Guy Fawkes - The guy who actually made it. It gives great satisfaction to me who's lived all his life in the UK to know that there was one guy who completely pissed on the upper echelons of the ruling class for years, devastating MI5 and MI6, and along with it the plans of imperial intrigue.

Prescott is more of a delinquent, a former junkie from a rough Scottish background, who's already pulled a gun in a police station and spent half his life in various institutions. He describes the gun incident thus;

"I was taking 8 grains of heroin and other drugs every day, and I sold all my personal possessions to buy them. I picked up a rich-looking character and stole a whole lot of stuff from him, including a gun. The same night I went to Piccadilly and tried to contact a pedlar, but got arrested. Drugs were costing me £10 a day. At the police station I was told to turn out my pockets and I pulled out the gun. A policeman shouted, 'Watch out, he's got a gun.' One dived under a table, the others stood up against the wall. I ran out of the room. The gun was loaded."

And so Prescott gets 5 $\frac{1}{2}$ years and ends up in Albany sharing a cell with Purdie, during his stretch for the Ulster Office petrol-bombing. (At their trial the police make a lot of the influence the intellectual Purdie has on Prescott. But, according to the beat poet Michael Kustow, Prescott is also a one-time ICA employee.)

CARR TROUBLE

1971: THE YEAR OF THE ANGRY BRIGADE - HEY DIG THE TIME IS RIGHT FOR VIOLENT REVOLUTION - ROBERT CARR GOT IT TONIGHT WE'RE GETTING CLOSER - HABERSHON - USUAL SUSPECTS - PUBLIC ENEMY NO. 1

JANUARY 1971: Cambridge students and lecturers strike over the banning and eventual deportation of German student leader Rudi Dutschke.

JANUARY 12: After thousands come out on strike and march through London against the Industrial Relations bill, two bombs explode at the Barnet home of Employment Minister Robert Carr. Following the first explosion at 10.05pm Carr takes his wife and daughter to a neighbour's. Then he tells his housekeeper to go back in and a second bomb goes off, at 10.20. The housekeeper isn't injured but three policemen are thrown to the ground by the blast. At the time of the explosions most of Scotland Yard's top brass are otherwise engaged, attending a special West End screening of '10 Rillington Place'. (The film of the career of Stuart Christie's namesake, John, the Notting Hill mass murderer.) 'Grandad' by Clive Dunn is top of the singles chart and 'Bridge over Troubled Waters' by Simon and Garfunkel is top of the album chart.

JANUARY 13: 'The Times', 'Guardian' and 'Mirror' receive Barnet post-marked letters containing the next communique;

Robert Carr got it tonight. We're getting closer. COMMUNIQUE 4. THE ANGRY BRIGADE.

The case comes under the jurisdiction of S Division of the Met, where Detective Chief Superintendent Roy Habershon, a former Fraud Squad officer, has just taken charge. Habershon sets about the investigations with some gusto but, once the top brass get back from the pictures, a Special Branch squad is formed to work full-time on the case as well. Justice Melford Stevenson, the 'Garden House Affair' judge (also known as the 'hanging judge'), is given a police guard after receiving a bomb threat; as is Ted Heath, environment minister Peter Walker, Hugh Fraser and most Cabinet ministers. These are angry times. Following the Carr bombings, 6 Conservative Party offices are petrol-bombed and 'The Daily Express' receives another communique;

The Angry Brigade are after Heath now. We're getting closer.

As press speculation reaches fever pitch - Is this the MPLA? UDA? IRA? - houses of 'known left-wing extremists' are raided all over London, causing not inconsiderable fear and loathing in both establishment and underground camps. The Notting Hill hippy scene comes in for particular police attention and a number of suspects are hauled up to Barnet for questioning (All are released without charge relating to the Carr bombs).
JANUARY 13/14: Police raids on Chris Reed in Tufnell Park and schools union activist, Stuart Roche. While the 'Evening Standard' announces that the police are after 'a young Scottish anarchist', who's been in prison in Spain. Obviously mean-

Robert Carr's gaff
in Hadley Green,
Barnet, after visit
from Angries.

ing Stuart Christie, though he isn't mentioned by name. As the rest of the press pick up on the lead a 'Scottish Daily Express' headline reads, 'Carr Bombs, Hunt for Scot'.

JANUARY 15: As the 'Daily Mirror' offers a reward of £10,000 for information leading to a conviction, Ian Purdie's brother, Robert is taken up to Barnet to be questioned about Ian. Meanwhile, Jim Greenfield gets nicked again, this time for dropping dud cheques in order to hire a car. He appears in court under the name 'Caddick' and gets off with a fine and conditional discharge.

JANUARY 16: Lisa Byer, a former girlfriend of Stuart Christie, is taken up to Barnet, where she claims Christie told her he was involved in a bombing campaign, wanted to use her as an alibi and showed her a clip of bullets in her car.

JANUARY 17: The Muswell Hill Agitprop shop and Ann Lamche of Cinema Action are raided. Address books are copied and more people taken off for questioning.

JANUARY 18: South African Airways office in Glasgow firebombed.

JANUARY 19: Jake Prescott gets pulled on Talbot Road in Notting Hill, 'on suspicion of possession of drugs'. As well as some dope he's found to be in possession of cheque books stolen from Oxford University. Because of his previous he's remanded in custody and sent down to Brixton. There, so the police story goes, he makes the mistake of confiding in his cell mates about the 'Miss World' and Carr bombs. This information duly finds it's way to Habershon, who discovers that Prescott's handwriting and the writing on the Carr communique envelopes are one and the same. Same day as the Prescott bust there are 4 more raids and Joe Keith and Tony Swash are questioned by Habershon.

JANUARY 20: Ian Purdie comes forward voluntarily, with proof that he was in Edinburgh at the time of the Carr bombing.

JANUARY 21: Paul Lewis of 'International Times' is questioned by Habershon and his home and the 'it' office are searched.

JANUARY 22: Chris Allen of Notting Hill People's Association is questioned by Edinburgh CID, prompting Habershon to take a 3 day sojourn north of the border.

JANUARY 23: Another raid in Edinburgh.

JANUARY 24: Back in London, but still in a Scottish vein, Stuart Christie's workmate Ross Flett and Phil Carver (of Bank of Bilbao fame) are raided and taken to Barnet for questioning. Special Branch Inspector Palmer-Hall, who's been following Christie's career for some time, conducts the raid and Habershon grills Flett back at Barnet, to not much avail. However, Christie's address book ('a glossary of international revolutionaries', according to Habershon) is acquired during the raid and John Barker's name crops up for the first time. Elsewhere in London two men are seized regarding the attacks on the Barclays banks, Conservative party offices and the MP Duncan Sandys. In the press, Christie officially becomes Public Enemy Number One, when 'The Times' reports;

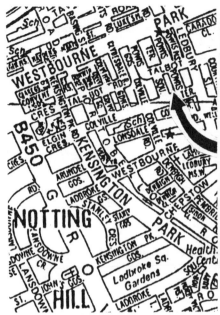

Jake Prescott

Nationwide police checks were being made last night to flush out a known bomb anarchist - a Scot in his early twenties whom the Special Branch have put at the top of their wanted list in connection with the double bombing of Employment Minister, Mr. Robert Carr. Suspect Number 1, who has haunts in Glasgow and London, is thought to have been behind a bomb blast at the London offices of the Spanish Iberia Airlines last August and also the planting of a device - it did not explode - on an Iberia Airliner at Heathrow.

Christie isn't named until Paul Foot attacks the press for hounding him in 'Private Eye', revealing his name in the process. Consequently, the press beseige the Harrow Gas Board yard where he works and Christie gives an interview to the 'Evening News' complaining about the police harassment he's been receiving. After that the 'Daily Express' report that he's gone underground in Paris and the police announce that they have 'no special interest' in him. According to 'The Christie File', during the Ross Flett interview, Habershon exclaims;

"You types make me fucking sick. You were talking to Christie. I can get Christie any time I want."

Habershon later admits that he always believed Christie to be 'instrumental to this large scale criminal conspiracy';

"I formed the view at that early stage that there existed in Britain a group of people of anti-Franco persuasion prepared to do bombing who had close contact with persons of similar mind on the continent, who themselves had access to French explosives. *(French Nitramite or Nitratex had been used in the 1st of May and the DEP bombs.)* Secondly that this group had either extended its aims to include demonstrations against such things as police and government and authority in this country, or had joined forces with a second group who had those aims, and thirdly that the series of bombings with these new aims were being carried out under the label of the Angry Brigade."

JANUARY 25: The home of the Lord Provost of Glasgow is fire-bombed.
JANUARY 27: The police are forced to admit that the earlier covered-up bombings did infact take place, when the Press Association receive another communique;

We are no mercenaries. We attack property not people. Carr, Rawlinson, Waldron, would all be dead if we had wished. Fascists and government agents are the only ones who attack the public - the fire-bombing of the West Indian party in South London, the West End cinema bomb. British democracy is based on more blood, terror, and exploitation than any empire in history. Has a brutal police force whose crimes against people the media will not report. Now its government has declared vicious class war. Carr's Industrial Relations Bill aims to make it a one-sided war. We have started to fight back and the war will be won by the organised working class, with bombs. COMMUNIQUE 5. THE ANGRY BRIGADE.

JANUARY 29: As a press black-out is imposed on the course of the investigations, 'The Times' announces;

Scotland Yard and security officials are becoming increasingly embarrassed and annoyed by the activities of the Angry Brigade, who cannot now be dismissed as a group of cranks. Some senior officers credit the group with a degree of professional skill that has seldom been experienced.

At the same time as the start of the Angry Brigade investigations, the world of football is still reeling from the Ibrox disaster and Special Branch/the press are also engaged in hounding Bobby Moore, regarding the Mexico World Cup jewellery theft incident. George Best has also fallen foul of the law. Other news includes a military coup in Uganda led by Idi Amin and Michael X doing a bunk to Trinidad.
JANUARY 30: Slough Conservative office firebombed and 'My Sweet Lord' by George Harrison knocks Clive Dunn's 'Grandad' off the No. 1 spot.

FEBRUARY 3: Jake Prescott is let out on bail and followed to 29 Grosvenor Avenue, Islington, another commune where he and Purdie have been staying. Which also happens to be the home of the women involved in the 'Miss World' flour-bombing and some members of the Kim Philby Dining Club, who are printing situ pamphlets on the premises.

FEBRUARY 6: The glorious striking print workers prevent Simon and Garfunkel from having a fifth week at the top of the album chart.

FEBRUARY 11: Habershon and the 'Barnet Brigade' disrupt the 'Miss World' flour-bombing trial at Bow Street and take 4 of the defendants (Sue Bradley, Jane Grant, Sarah Martin and Sarah Wilson) off to Barnet to be questioned. (The National Council for Civil Liberties subsequently complains to the Home Secretary that this was against 'Judges' Rules' and charge the police with false imprisonment and assault.) At the same time police raid Grosvenor Avenue for explosives and take away address books, diaries and assorted revolutionary literature. Then Jake Prescott is picked up again at the Weavers Arms on Newington Green Road, with a Dutchman, Jan Oudenaarden, and taken to Barnet to be held without access to solicitors for 2 days. Habershon remarks, "I am not concerned with legal niceties."

FEBRUARY 11-13: Prescott denies anything to do with the bombings, but gets into a bit of a mess under interrogation. His slip-ups lead to a raid on Barker and Creek's place in Moss Side, and the further implication of Ian Purdie.

FEBRUARY 13: Manchester police raid 14 Cannock Street for explosives. As with all the other raids, they don't find any but Barker, Creek, Chris Bott and Kate McLean duly come into the frame and have their address books, letters, typewriter, etc, seized. Meanwhile back in London, Oudenaarden and Prescott's lawyers invoke Habeus Corpus to get them released or charged. The Dutchman is released, but Jake Prescott is charged with conspiracy to cause explosions, between July 30 1970 and December 1971; and specifically with the Carr, DEP and Miss World bombings. 'Frendz' #10 (38) reports;

Habershon tries to prevent access to Jake - defence lawyer complains of scandalous abuse of police powers - commotion in court - several adjournments - Habershon is cross examined in the witness box for 'grounds of arrest' - Chief Supt. H asks for legal advice is shit scared and guess what? He asks to see a lawyer. Habie is accused of attempting to induce Jake to change his lawyer - the good pig denies it. Jake shouts out loud, real loud "YOU LIAR!"

FEBRUARY 15: Cannock Street raided again.

FEBRUARY 16: The Communist paper, 'Red Mole', publishes a message to; *'All members of the Angry Brigade: The man known to you as Duncan is a pig. The man who went to Manchester before 12 January is a pig. Ask yourselves, are you being used by the pigs?'* According to Stuart Christie this is just a communist or

Trotskyist wind-up, but 'the man who went to Manchester' is Ian Purdie (for a Claimant's Union conference).

FEBRUARY 19: Habershon goes to Edinburgh again to follow up a lead that Prescott has corresponded with a girl now living in the city. While he's there he checks out the local anarchist scene; 2 houses are raided and Chris and Jane Allen are questioned. Back in London, Habershon subsequently tracks down one Irene Jamieson, who says she was engaged to Prescott until Purdie and Jerry Osner turned him into an anarchist. Same day, a local Essex paper gets a call from an 'Angry Brigade spokesman' who says the next campaign will be aimed at Conservative party policy regarding South Africa. And 'The Times' publishes the next communique;

FELLOW REVOLUTIONARIES... We have sat quietly and suffered the violence of the system for too long. We are being attacked daily. Violence does not only exist in the army, the police and prisons. It exists in the shoddy alienating culture pushed out by TV films and magazines, it exists in the ugly sterility of urban life. It exists in the daily exploitation of our Labour, which gives big Bosses the power to control our lives and run the system for their own ends. How many Rolls Royces... how many Northern Irelands... how many anti-Trade Union bills will it take to demonstrate that in a crisis of capitalism the ruling class can only react by attacking the people politically? But the system will never collapse or capitulate by itself. More and more workers now realise this and are transforming union consciousness into offensive political militancy. In one week, one million workers were on strike... Fords, Post Office, BEA, oil delivery workers... Our role is to deepen the political contradictions at every level. We will not achieve this by concentrating on 'issues' or by using watered down socialist platitudes. In Northern Ireland the British Army and its minions has found a practising range: the CS gas and bullets in Belfast will be in Derby and Dagenham tomorrow.

OUR attack is violent... Our violence is organised. The question is not whether the revolution will be violent. Organised militant struggle and organised terrorism go side by side. These are the tactics of the revolutionary class movement. Where two or three revolutionaries use organised violence to attack the class system... there is the Angry Brigade. Revolutionaries all over England are already using the name to publicise their attacks on the system. No revolution was ever won without violence. Just as the structures and programmes of a new revolutionary society must be incorporated into every organised base at every point in the struggle, so must organised violence accompany every point of the struggle until, armed the revolutionary working class overthrows the capitalist system. COMMUNIQUE 6. THE ANGRY BRIGADE.

FEBRUARY 20: The raids continue; Today it's Mike Kane's turn.

FEBRUARY 27: Barker, Creek, Greenfield and Mendelson attend a meeting in Liverpool to launch 'Strike', a Scouse 'alternative to the underground press'. Over the next few months the 4 all contribute articles (including 'The Repression Industry' by Greenfield and Mendelson) and jointly edit the Judges and the Law section. Immediately after the meeting Greenfield, Mendelson and some others drive to Widnes, Greenfield's home town, and stop at a pub. A local finds them suspicious and calls the police, who bust the group for speed, dope and a stolen cheque book from Essex University. They all give false names and addresses and are bailed to Colchester police station.

MARCH 4: Habershon receives a tip-off that Ian Purdie has been seen at an address in Battersea.

MARCH 5: Another raid on another house on Talbot Road, Notting Hill.

MARCH 6: Ian Purdie is duly arrested after a raid on a house in Tyneham Road, Battersea. Purdie does a runner but is apprehended on some wasteground outback of the house. Habershon announces; "The raid was to find explosives and Ian Purdie. They are synonymous as far as I am concerned."

MARCH 7: Purdie says nothing under interrogation but nonetheless he's charged, along with Prescott and 'others', with 'conspiring to cause explosions likely to endanger life and cause serious injury to property'. Purdie and Prescott are put in the top security wing at Brixton, as class A prisoners, which means they're confined to their cells 23 hours a day.

**Ian Purdie. Synonymous
with explosives**

POWER TO THE PEOPLE

IT'S FORD TONIGHT - GANTS HILL - AND IT FLASHED WE WERE INVINCIBLE - THE IRA CONNECTION - THE CHEQUE FRAUD - THE SITUATIONIST COP - POLICE SMASH ANARCHIST BOMB GANG

MARCH 10: 'The Guardian' runs an article on excesses in police investigations. MARCH 18: Now questions are asked in the House. Clinton Davis queries Home Secretary Reginald Maudling about the increasingly frequent raids. So far 25 people have been taken up to Barnet but none of them have been charged. The police are also accused of denying suspects access to solicitors and using explosives warrants indiscriminatley. Habershon subsequently makes his first report to the Director of Public Prosecutions, recommending that the charge of conspiracy to cause explosions should encompass 14 attacks; from the 1st of May Spanish Embassy in March 1968 up to the Carr bombing. To illustrate his case he now has a chart drawn up by forensics expert, Howard Yallop, linking the various bombs

together. On the same day a man attempts to rob a bank in London with a bomb, that turns out to be a tin filled with coal.

MARCH 19: Habershon's list is extended when a massive explosion wrecks the Ford Motor Company Offices at Gants Hill, Ilford. That night there's apparently a lot of coming and going down Grosvenor Avenue. The attack coincides with a nationwide Ford workers' strike and the next communique-cum-Angry Brigade manifesto appears soon after;

COMRADES! Two months ago we blew up Carr's house. Revolutionary violence through the high walls of English liberalism. Apart from a short communique we remained silent since... Why?... who is the Angry Brigade... what are its political objectives... a lot of criticism was directed toward vague directions... they called us the Special Branch, the Front, Anarcho-nuts, Commies, Bomb-mob, the lot... we believe that the time has come for an honest dialogue... with any comrade who cares to address us... through the Underground press... through anything. Look around you brother and sister... look at the barriers... don't breathe... don't love, don't strike, don't make trouble... DON'T.

The politicians, the leaders, the rich, the big bosses, are in command... THEY control. WE, THE PEOPLE, SUFFER... THEY have tried to make us mere functions of a production process. THEY have polluted the world with chemical waste from their factories. THEY shoved garbage from their media down our throats. THEY made us absurd sexual caricatures, all of us, men and women. THEY killed, napalmed, burned us into soap, mutilated us, raped us. It's gone on for centuries.

Slowly we started understanding the BIG CON. We saw that they had defined 'our possibilities'. They said: You can demonstrate... between police lines. You can have sex... in the normal position and as commodity; commodities are good. You can rally in defence of the TUC... The 'leadership' is wise.

THEY used confusing words like 'public' or the 'National Interest'. Is the Public some kind of 'Dignified Body' which we belong to, only until we go on strike? Why are we reduced then to dreaded scroungers, ruining the country's economy? Is 'National Interest' anything more than THEIR interest?

Lately we started seeing through another kind of con: There is a certain kind of professional who claims to represent us... the MPs, the Communist Party, the Union leaders, the Social Workers, the old-old left... All these people presumed to act on our behalf. All these people have certain things in common... THEY are all afraid of us... THEY'LL preach towards keeping the peace... and we are bored... poor... and very tired of keeping the peace.

THE ANGRY BRIGADE BECAME A REALITY. We knew that every moment of badly paid boredom in a production line was a violent crime. We had rejected all the senile hierarchies and ALL the structures, the liars, the poverty pimps, the Carrs, the Jacksons, the Rawlinsons, the Bob Hopes, the Waldrons...To believe that OUR struggle could be restricted to the channels provided to us by the pigs, WAS THE GREATEST CON. And we started hitting them.

January 12 was important... we shattered the blackouts of the yellow press... hundreds of years of Imperialism... millions of victims of colonisation were breaking up... all the suppressed frustration, all the glow of unleashed energy was blowing our minds... Carr was totally unimportant... he was just a symbol... we could have killed the bastard... or Powell or Davies... or any pig.

Then we were scared... like any newly born baby opening our eyes to a gigantic glow - we got frightened... every knock, every word became a menace... but simultaneously we realised that our panic was minute compared to the panic of the Mirrors and the Habershons AND IT FLASHED: WE WERE INVINCIBLE... because we were everybody.

THEY COULD NOT JAIL US FOR WE DID NOT EXIST. We started daring out into the open, talking to friends, to neighbours, to people in the pubs, in football games... and we knew we were not alone... WE WERE ALIVE AND GROWING!

COMRADES! Brothers and sisters we hardly know have been picked up, framed, intimidated, harassed. The McCarthys, the Prescotts, the Purdies are all INNOCENT. The pigs need scapegoats. Our power is the 6 Conservative Offices petrol bombed on January 13, the Altringham generator which was blown out are all answers of the Revolutionary movement to our call.

We are certain that every single day that these comrades stay behind bars will be avenged... Even if it means that some of the Pigs will lose their lives.

Three weeks ago we nearly blew up Jackson's headquarters. We knew he had to sell out. We wanted to hit him BEFORE he did the damage. But inside us we carry the remnants of liberalism and irrationality... burdens of our past we have tried to shed. He beat us to it... HE SOLD OUT... Let the working brothers and sisters be our jury. This time we knew better: it's FORD TONIGHT. We are celebrating the hundred years of the Paris Commune. We are celebrating our REVOLUTION which won't be controlled.

Our revolution is autonomous rank and file action - we create it OURSELVES. We have confidence now... we don't have to wait for them to dangle something tempting like a Powell, a Bill, or a bad apple in front of our faces, before we jump like rabbits. We don't clutch desperately at the illusion of FREEDOM. Our strategy is clear: How can we smash the system? How can the people take power?

We must ATTACK, we cannot delegate our desire to take the offensive. Sabotage is a reality... getting out of the factory is not the only way to strike... stay in and take over. We are against any external structure, whether it's called Carr, Jackson, CP or SLL is irrelevant - they're all one and the same.

WE BELIEVE IN THE AUTONOMOUS WORKING CLASS. WE ARE PART OF IT. AND WE ARE READY TO GIVE OUR LIVES FOR OUR LIBERATION. POWER TO THE PEOPLE. COMMUNIQUE 7. THE ANGRY BRIGADE.

MARCH 19/20: Another series of raids, mostly around Notting Hill on anyone connected with Purdie and Prescott. Powis Square 8 defence documents perused by SB Chief Supt. Curtis during raid on Talbot Road. John Lennon's 'Power to the People' enters the charts. 'Hot Love' by T. Rex at No. 1.

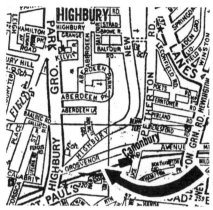

MARCH 23: 29 Grosvenor Avenue raided again and searched extensively with sniffer dogs. During the raid a girl pulls up outside in a Volkswagen, which is included in the search. A key found in the car turns out to belong to a left-luggage locker at Euston, where more stolen cheque books and papers belonging to a German, Wolf Seeberg are discovered. Seeberg subsequently calls the police to ask for his car back and the call is traced to the Andersonstown home of IRA leaders, Jerry and Rita O'Hare.

MARCH 24: A girl is arrested after walking into a police trap at the Euston left-luggage locker. Same day, two more raids in East London on the homes of Ron Bailey and Digger Walsh (an anarchist accredited with the Carr bombing in the French magazine, 'Politique Hebdo'), by Cremer 'the Situationist Cop' and Bentley of the 'Barnet Brigade', with explosives warrants.

LATE MARCH: After the girl arrested at Euston is charged with dishonest handling and let out on bail, the RUC raid the O'Hares in Andersonstown and find Wolf Seeberg in bed with the Euston girl. Seeberg is brought back to London and charged with cheque fraud at Albany Street.

Habershon might not have been getting anywhere with the actual Angry Brigade investigations but at his speciality, fraud he's starting to uncover a pretty juicy conspiracy. According to Gordon Carr the police are totally confused by the political dimension of the case and the hippy commune scene they're getting into and wouldn't have got anywhere with it, if they hadn't stumbled across some orthodox crime. The cheque-books have mostly been stolen from Cambridge, Essex and Oxford Universities, on a fairly vast scale. Cheques had then been forged and 'cross-fired' between relating accounts and PO savings books, also stolen in large quantities. Habershon has the police lab at Holborn matching up handwriting samples from his and the SB political suspects list with the forged cheques as they come in from all round the country. According to Habershon;

"It was evident that these persons and their associates whose identities I was learning were and had been for some time wholly engaged in revolutionary political activities of various sorts and that the majority had no visible means of income. It was a reasonable assumption to come to that they were subsidising and financing their various activities from the proceeds of fraud."

Habershon's fraud inquiries become all-consuming, reducing the Special Branch boys to the demeaning role of passing on fraud info to his Barnet team. But in the end they're allowed to return to some political policing and Habershon gets his own Fraud Squad at New Scotland Yard, led by Detective Inspector George Mould.

MARCH 30: Following a botched petrol-bomb attack on Queens University, Belfast, the RUC arrest an underground press contingent, including Felix de Mendelsohn (of 'Suck' fame), Jill Marcuson (the wife of 'Friends' editor Alan) and future Sex Pistols photographer, Joe Stevens; under the command of phoney IRA member/dope smuggler Jim McCann. The resulting 'Evening News' headline, 'Police Smash Anarchist Bomb Gang', has everybody back in London thinking the Angry Brigade's been busted. According to David Leigh in 'High Time (The Life and Times of Howard Marks' - Jim McCann's dope-smuggling co-hort/Welsh counter-culture icon);

Watching the Detective: The Situationist cop Cremer visiting 'Time Out'.

THE ANGRY BRIGADE

(The Angry Brigade) had connections with the Underground press and Scotland Yard frequently (and mistakenly) used to raid the premises of IT looking for them. Infact, their sympathisers were later to be found among the political activists and 'street hippies' who clustered round 'Friends' (on Portobello Road) the following year, after Marcuson left it. But police never realised this.

APRIL 1: The house of the headmaster of Roydale School is firebombed. More houses in Notting Hill are raided and Powis Square 8 defence documents are seized. During these raids Sergeant Cremer unearths John Barker's copy of 'Society of the Spectacle' (with notes in his hand-writing) in a Powis Square basement flat. Thus putting Barker in the frame for the recent Situationist inspired communiques, as far as Cremer's concerned anyway. Cremer is described as a bit of a 'Rosie Bloom' from 'Performance' type, straight but with an understanding of the bohemian world. Or so he thinks. According to Stuart Christie, at this stage Special Branch are betting on him, Habershon on Purdie and Prescott, and Cremer is playing the Situationist wildcard;

John's circle, however, afforded a chance to synthesize the rival theories about the background of the Angry Brigade. Most of them were young, in revolt against what they called 'the work ethic' as well as bourgeois convention. They lived in communes and never woke up in the morning - everything most repellent to tight-arsed detectives, who came fresh from examining the books fiddled by bowler-hatted businessmen to plunge into the murky world of the underground. Yet these young people were no drop-outs politically...

APRIL 5: A bomb is left in Leicester Square and an arson attempt is made on Gosport Conservative Club.

APRIL 15: Jake Prescott is (formally) presented with three more charges (on top of his original dope and fraud charges); conspiring with Purdie to cause explosions 'with others' between July 1970 and March 1971; and actually executing the Miss World and DEP bombings.

APRIL 22: Committal proceedings against Purdie and Prescott finally begin at Barnet. The two have been kept in solitary confinement at Brixton since their arrest, evidence of arrest has been withheld and £10 grand bail is refused by the Barnet magistrate. Prescott's brief, Arnold Rosen says, "Words fail me to describe the outrageous use of police power," and successfully applies to have detectives removed from court during proceedings. Same day there's an arson attack on the Whitechapel Barclays Bank.

APRIL 23: A letter bomb is discovered addressed to an MP at the House of Commons. And during an apparent drugs raid in Wivenhoe, Essex, suspects are shown photos of Jim Greenfield and Anna Mendelson.

APRIL 26: On the night of the Everton/Liverpool Cup semi-final at Old Trafford, Cannock Street is raided for the third time and Chris Bott is arrested on fraud charges. He's taken to Brixton and charged, then released on bail.

APRIL 27: 'Frendz' #10 (38) report on Purdie and Prescott committal proceedings:

Barnet Court - Bumbleshon in the witness box, Purdie's counsel Sedley asking questions.
Habershon: "Yes, I gave instructions for Purdie to be arrested."
Sedley: "And you also gave instructions for a search warrant for explosives for the same address." (Tyneham Rd.)
Habershon: "Yes."
Sedley: "What were you really looking for? Explosives or Purdie?"
Habershon: "They were synonymous."
Sedley: "But you didn't find any explosives, so are they still synonymous?"
Habershon: "Yes."

APRIL 28: 'The Times' receives a liquid bomb through the post; **From the Vengeance Squad, the Angry Brigade, the People's Army. We will use these. Many of them in June and July. Revolution now.**

APRIL 29: Berkeley Nuclear Power Station sabotaged. Third such case in 3 months. More raids on International Socialists printers and members, and Agitprop again.

BLOW IT UP
BURN IT DOWN
KICK IT TILL IT BREAKS

BIBA'S - IF YOU'RE NOT BUSY BEING BORN YOU'RE BUSY BUYING - LIFE IS SO BORING - WE'VE JUST DONE THE POLICE COMPUTER - GUNS IN THEIR POCKETS AND HATRED IN THEIR MINDS - JOHN DILLON'S IN - PUT THE BOOT IN - COMMANDER X AND THE BOMB SQUAD - NASTY TALES AND OZ

MAY 1: The next bomb attack goes straight for the Spectacular Society and splits the undergound scene down the middle. As an affectionate Up Yours to the traditional Left, the Angry Brigade choose May Day to blow up Biba's Boutique in Kensington High Street. Thus alienating the political and fashion wings of the underground from each other. The accompanying communique reads;

IF YOU'RE NOT BUSY BEING BORN, YOU'RE BUSY BUYING.

All the sales girls in the flash boutiques are made to dress the same and have the same make-up, representing the 1940s. In fashion as in everything else, capitalism can only go backwards - they've nowhere to go - they're dead.

The future is ours. Life is so boring there is nothing to do except spend all our wages on the latest skirt or shirt.

Brothers and Sisters, what are your real desires? Sit in the drugstore, look distant, empty, bored, drinking some tasteless coffee? Or perhaps BLOW IT UP or BURN IT DOWN. The only thing you can do with modern slave-houses - called boutiques - is WRECK THEM. You can't reform profit capitalism and inhumanity. Just KICK IT TILL IT BREAKS.

REVOLUTION. COMMUNIQUE 8. THE ANGRY BRIGADE.

51

It takes the New York Dolls, who play at Biba's Rainbow Room in 1973, to bring underground politics and fashion back together again. At the time of the Biba's bomb, the Dolls' future manager, Malcolm McLaren is failing to complete a psychogeographical film about Oxford Street and just about to quit Goldsmith's College of Art. By the end of 1971 he has his own boutique at 430 Kings Road.

MAY 4: An unexploded bomb is found attached to the underside of Lady Beaverbrook's car (Stuart Christie considers this one to be either a mistake or not an AB bomb). Home-made bombs are also found near Sidcup and Chislehurst Grammar School, where Ted Heath has just received the Freedom of Bexley. Police search now spans Kent, Essex and Oxfordshire.
MID-MAY: Police siege of the Metro Youth Club on Tavistock Road, Notting Hill results in another W11/West Indian/counter-culture trial. Stones 'Sticky Fingers' replaces 'Motown Chartbusters' at top of album chart.
MAY 22: 3 weeks after Biba's, the Press Association receive a call; "This is the Angry Brigade. We've just done the police computer." Which is situated at Tintagel House, on the Embankment. Simultaneously 3 bombs go off in Paris, at the British Rail offices, a Rolls Royce showroom and a supplier of Land-Rovers. These are accompanied by an open letter to Ted Heath (who's in Paris at the time on Common Market business) from a coalition of the IRSM / First of May / Angry Brigade / Group Commune 71 and Groupe Marius Jacob, protesting about the Common Market and the treatment of Purdie and Prescott.
    The Tintagel House bomb is accompanied by the snappy, pro-situ Angry Brigade Communique 9;

We are getting closer. We are slowly destroying the long tentacles of the oppressive State machine... secret files in the universities, work study in the factories, the census at home, social security files, computers, TV, Giro, passports, work permits, insurance cards. Bureaucracy and technology used against the people... to speed up our work, to slow down our minds and actions, to obliterate the truth. Police computers cannot tell the truth. They just record our 'crimes'. The pig murders go unrecorded. Stephen McCarthy, Peter Savva, David Owale - The murder of these brothers is not written on any card. We will avenge our brothers. If they murder another brother or sister, pig blood will flow in the streets. 168 explosions last year, hundreds of threatening phonecalls to government, bosses, leaders...
    THE ANGRY BRIGADE IS THE MAN OR WOMAN SITTING NEXT TO YOU. THEY HAVE GUNS IN THEIR POCKETS AND HATRED IN THEIR MINDS. WE ARE GETTING CLOSER. OFF THE SYSTEM AND ITS PROPERTY. POWER TO THE PEOPLE. COMMUNIQUE 9. THE ANGRY BRIGADE

MAY 27: Ian Purdie and Jake Prescott are committed for trial at the Old Bailey. 'Frendz' #10 (38) describes their committal proceedings thus;

THE UNSOPHISTICATED WORKING LAD AND THE SCHEMING ANARCHIST

Hudson QC, lawyer for Ian Purdie told the magistrate at Barnet, "There is not a shred of evidence for this man to stand trial." The case against Jake is built up on a number of alleged statements that he is said to have made to the police, and his conversations with 2 prisoners who shared a cell with him while he was on remand in Brixton for the cheque bouncing offences. It is important to bear in mind that the police are trying to cultivate the impression that Jake was an unsophisticated working class lad who had been indoctrinated by the clever calculating Purdie. To this end, the statements which Purdie is alleged to have made to Habershon sound almost genuine: the cynical distrust of the police which might be expected from anyone with an understanding of the workings of justice and the law. Thus;

'Mr. Habershon said that he had said the Albert Hall explosion appeared to have been connected with the Women's Liberation Movement, and Mr. Purdie had told him, "I suppose you are going to infer that, because I have friends in Women's Lib, I did it for them. You must be out of your tiny mind." And again. 'Referring to the explosion at Mr. Carr's house, he asked Mr. Purdie: "Have you any connection with those responsible?" Mr. Purdie allegedly replied; "Look, do you often sit here talking to yourself? There is too much shit coming out. If you think I did it, why don't you charge me?"' The Times, April 28.

Compare this with the conversation Habershon said he had with Jake. (Suggestions as to which TV script it was taken from to Commander Bond, Tintagel House...) Talking about the conversations which Jake is alleged to have had with his cell mates, Habershon allegedly asked: "Did you tell them these things?" Jake: "Perhaps I did, but I was only spinning them a fanny." And later. H: "What do you want to say?" J: "I know Ian Purdie knows who did the Carr bombing." "How do you know this?" "He told me in a pub. He mentioned the

People's Association of Notting Hill. He spoke about Grosvenor Avenue... They kicked him out because they reckoned he was a terrorist." "At noon it is proposed to charge you with the Carr bombing. Do you wish to say anything more?" "Why should I say anything about it? I will either go to prison on my own or with other people. If I am done, I'm done. I can't see any profit in putting the others in it."

Anyone who has read some of Jake's letters from solitary confinement in Brixton Prison will realise just how artificial a picture of him the pigs are trying to create. The evidence of the prisoner Mr. A is equally unrealistic. According to Mr. A Jake went into some detail about how he and 3 others had blown up Robert Carr's house, including details about the way the bomb was manufactured. Mr. B, the other man in the cell who was supposed to join the roadshow, didn't agree. He was granted bail shortly after agreeing to give evidence against Jake. He jumped bail and wasn't available unfortunately. Mr. A appeared in court badly beaten up. He had been transferred from Brixton to Wandsworth, where he was in voluntary solitary confinement. People's justice had been exercised even before he told his story.

The rest of the evidence against Jake, apart from friends who didn't say what the prosecutor had said they would, came from the handwriting expert. He was to give evidence that the writing on 2 of the envelopes containing communiques was Jakes. Infact he admitted that he 'couldn't be sure'. It took 11 days (spread out between the 22nd of April and 27th May) to give this non-evidence. The trial at the Old Bailey promises to be an even longer elaboration of a web of innuendo, doubt-ful circumstantial evidence, and trial by political belief. In a letter to the outside, Ian Purdie spelt it out;

'I think that those of you who are on the outside should invite many more people to attend the hearings. The newspapers, of course, give a very misleading impression as to the tenor of the proceedings. People must come to understand what is going on. There exist too large a number of citizens who have little idea of the games they are playing. They should see that the State seeks to put a person's thoughts and beliefs on trial. They say a person with strong anarchistic (sic) views literally indoctrinated another in the space of a couple of months. They will bring persons to testify to this who do not know a conservative from a trotskyist. They will bring them to lie manifestly, they will bring senior officials from the police department to elucidate the monumental works of the script-writing department of the Department of Public Prosecutions. They will produce books and documents they have seized. It is important that much of this should be witnessed. It's beauti-ful to see the effect it has on people in here. Guys tap you on the shoulder and ask if you're OK for tobacco. I hear people talking about Messrs. A & B and laughing like hell at the transparent absurdity of the case before us - that much they see even from the papers.'

All the evidence suggests that there is no connection between Ian Purdie, Jake

Prescott... and the Angry Brigade, except that Ian & Jake are real ANGRY about being framed up because Scotland Yard picked them out of the hat as the most likely candidates.

JUNE 1: 'The Times' receives another communique;

If Heath and Rippon contrive to enter the Common Market without seeking the opinion of the British people they will be on the receiving end of a bullet. This is no idle threat. Signed: The Angry Brigade.

JUNE 11: Purdie and Prescott charged with conspiracy to defraud, along with Anna Mendelson and 3 others. Mendelson and Greenfield are now listed as wanted persons and their pictures appear in the 'Police Gazette'.

JUNE 22: At the height of a dispute in Liverpool between Ford and militant shop steward John Dillon, the Essex home of Ford Chairman William Batty and the Ford Dagenham Plant are both visited by the Angries and left suitably bombed. Communique 10;

JOHN DILLON'S IN; WE WON. BATTY AND HIS TRANSFORMER'S OUT; WE WON AGAIN. PUT THE BOOT IN. BOGSIDE - CLYDESIDE. SUPPORT THE ANGRY SIDE. SPREAD THE WORD. POWER TO THE PEOPLE. COMMUNIQUE 10. THE ANGRY BRIGADE.

Sir John Waldron subsequently calls a meeting at New Scotland Yard to pass on the message from Ted Heath that; 'the Angry Brigade must be found and smashed. We have been ordered to treat the Angry Brigade as Public Enemy Number 1. This is a top priority job.'

It's now that 'The Bomb Squad' is formed, to ward off criticism in the press and to relieve the original Barnet team. Habershon is demoted to Number 2 and, along with his files and personnel, transferred to New Scotland Yard. There North London divisional chief, Commander Ernest Bond takes charge of a 40 strong squad working full-time on the case. Two thirds are Special Branch, with Habershon's one third normal CID now in the minority. Bond's identity is kept secret and he becomes known as 'Commander X', the mysterious supremo brought in to crack the Angry Brigade, answerable only to the Cabinet itself. Or as Peter Gladstone Smith puts it in the 'Sunday Telegraph';

YARD WILL GET THE ANGRY BRIGADE

A special team of 20 hand-picked detectives from the Flying Squad and Special Branch, working with army bomb disposal experts and Home Office scientists.

Their leader, a commander, whose name is being kept secret for his own safety, is known as rough and ready. The squad is taking a tough line. It will raid hippy communes, question avowed members of the 'underground' and build up a complete file on the sub-culture that threatens the present social order.

The state of play when Commander Bond takes over is; Purdie and Prescott in the slammer, indefinitely awaiting trial; Chris Bott, on bail for fraud; Stuart Christie, apparently in the clear; John Barker, Hilary Creek, Jim Greenfield and Anna Mendelson coming into the frame. 'Chirpy Chirpy Cheap Cheap' by Middle of the Road is No. 1.

JUNE 23: The 'Oz' obscenity trial begins in Number Two Court of the Old Bailey. Jim Anderson, Felix Dennis and Richard Neville stand accused of conspiring to corrupt the morals of young children, with the 'Schoolkids' issue of 'Oz'. As the Glastonbury Free Festival is somewhat overshadowed by the Christian revival Festival of Light, the publishers of 'The Little Red Schoolbook' and Compendium bookshop (regarding Bill Levy's 'Suck') are also up on obscenity charges and copies of the underground comic 'Nasty Tales' are seized.

**395 Amhurst Road,
Stoke Newington.**

MOONLIGHTERS CELL

AMHURST ROAD - DAVIES IS A LYING BASTARD - BOGSIDE - CLYDESIDE - JOIN THE ANGRY SIDE - LAST TANGO IN PARIS - MOONLIGHTERS CELL - POINT YOUR GUN - THE STAKEOUT - THE BUST - INTERESTING ARSENAL - HAPPINESS IS A WARM GUN

'Extremism is going beyond the point when the guy who's been exploiting you for years says a joke is a joke, this is going too far. It's kicking the capitalist when he's down, as he screams you're not playing the game, when he's never played the game, never in his whole fucking life.'

(Anon. From papers seized at Amhurst Road)

JULY 3: Jim Morrison dies in Paris.

JULY 4: Barker, Creek, Greenfield and Mendelson rent the top floor flat at 395 Amhurst Road, Stoke Newington (under assumed names from stolen cheque-books). Here the 4 keep a low profile, but continue to work on, amongst other things; a pro-situ unitary urbanist analysis of the Housing Finance Bill and Purdie and Prescott's defence campaign, which includes a 'Whose Conspiracy?' flyposting campaign.

JULY 15: West German police shoot dead RAF member Petra Schelm.

JULY 19: A factory at Dordan is damaged by fires started by several incendiary devices.

JULY 26: Ian Purdie refused bail of £17,500 by Judge Melford Stevenson.

JULY 28: Stuart Christie visits Amhurst Road with the latest issue of 'Black Flag' and goes out for a drink with John Barker. Christie says that, unknown to him, by now Barker and co. have been contacted by Angry Brigade representatives; regarding their work on the Housing Finance Bill and Purdie and Prescott's defence.

JULY 31: Despite round-the-clock police protection the London home of John Davies, Secretary of State for Trade and Industry, is badly damaged by a powerful

57

explosion. The bomb is placed outside Davies' Hurlingham apartment in a gift-wrapped box and slightly injures an inquisitive neighbour. Davies has just announced the closure of the Upper Clydeside shipbuilding yard. 'The Times' reports; *'This latest incident has seriously embarrassed senior Scotland Yard officers.'* As the accompanying communique again almost pleads with the workers of the Bogside and Clydeside, workers everywhere to join with the Angry Side;

DAVIES IS A LYING BASTARD. He hides the deliberate rundown of heavy industry, the rundown of investment in the traditionally depressed areas, that's never been much anyway, by saying that the closures at UCS are just the result of bad management. And the bloody management won't suffer anyway. The conditions he's made for the new company are tough only for the workers who have to sign once and for all a contract they can't fight according to the Industrial Relations Bill.

Davies 'courageously' says the government won't support lame ducks. Yet 2 weeks ago the government put a massive investment in Harland and Wolff. A political move to keep capitalism going at any cost in the face of the people's uprising. VICTORY TO THE WORKERS ON CLYDESIDE. We'd like to say to you to watch out for all the vultures who'll be flying to Clydeside to tell you what to do. The same people who signed the productivity deals that started the redundancy ball rolling are now trying to feed off your struggle. If there's going to be an occupation it's got to be for real. Take the yards from the bosses and keep them. The Labour Party, the Unions and their minions, the CP with its productivity craze, the same bastards who always sell us out, will try to fob you off with gestures like one day strikes and one day occupations, petitions, etc, which will achieve bugger all.

YOU ARE YOUR OWN LEADERS. HAVE YOUR OWN TACTICS. CONTROL YOUR OWN STRUGGLE - SOLIDARITY. BOGSIDE, CLYDESIDE, JOIN THE ANGRY SIDE. COMMUNIQUE 11. THE ANGRY BRIGADE.

AUGUST 2: 'Oz' trial judge Argyle receives bomb threats, that turn out to be concocted by the wife of a court official, because she's nervous about Argyle coming to dinner (according to 'Oz' editor Richard Neville). Trial date for Purdie and Prescott set for September 7 and more raids, including places in Essex and the Agitprop bookshop/commune in Bethnal Green. During the latter Habershon, who's just been voted 'Pig of the Year' in the underground press, seizes Purdie and Prescott defence material, with a view to making a contempt case out of it. The Agitprop collective apply to the High court to get the stuff returned but Habershon's seizure is upheld.

AUGUST 5: Judge Argyle sentences the 'Oz' editorship to 9-15 months/deportation for publishing/posting obscene material. As Argyle's effigy is burnt outside the Old Bailey, Richard Neville comes up with his famous quote, that there's an inch of difference between a Conservative and a Labour Government, but in that inch the Underground survived. The next issue of 'Oz' is sub-titled the 'Angry Oz'. (For the record, the sentences are lifted by the Appeal Court in November.)

AUGUST 15: Following the latest round of raids there's another bombing at an army recruiting office in Holloway. This is the last attack officially attributed to the Angry Brigade. But it's only the beginning of yet more raids. According to 'Frendz', Home Secretary Reginald Maudling personally instructs Sir John Waldron and Commander Bond to 'take some firm action'.

AUGUST 16: Bethnal Green Agitprop raided again for explosives. Meanwhile, Hilary Creek sets off for Paris, allegedly to call upon 1st of May for assistance in a kidnapping (in order to spring Purdie and Prescott). In Paris, the police claim, she goes to Maubert-Mutualite metro station to meet 1st of May contact Garcia Calvo, a university Latin lecturer, and receives 33 sticks of gelignite at Calvo's pad off Boulevard St. Germain. Creek claims the purpose of her trip is merely to set up a news information service in the Latin Quarter. However, according to John Barker, later that afternoon the two representatives of the Angry Brigade return to Amhurst Road and ask him to go to France to translate for a girl, who's going to meet 1st of

Anna Mendelson and Hilary Creek. Revolutionary Babes.

May representatives (regarding Purdie and Prescott). Barker writes out the following message;

These are our tactics for the trial. If he gets sent down we'd want to get him out, are you interested? We don't think kidnapping will work. Springing them is one way, the other is a carefully guarded series of actions and threats together. If we did a kidnapping we would also demand the release of, say, someone put in prison for the Industrial Relations Bill.

Stuart Christie says Barker's original reason for going to Paris is to see Guy Debord, to get permission to translate 'Society of the Spectacle' into English. There's also some talk of doing a French version of the Claimants' Union and 'Strike'.

AUGUST 17: Habershon and Special Branch DCI Riby Wilson unearth another communique when they raid 90 Talbot Road, headquarters of the Notting Hill People's Association, with a stolen goods warrant. 'The Moonlighters Cell Communique', as it becomes known (named in honour of the 19th Century Irish revolutionary, Captain Moonlight), is obviously aimed at the introduction of Stormont's new powers of internment in Northern Ireland and to back up the Holloway bomb;

Over 5,500 refugees, 2,000 homeless, over 20 dead in 2 days, 230 imprisoned without charge or trial, the six occupied counties of Ireland are terrorised by gunmen in khaki. This war of terror is carried out in the name of the British people. THIS IS A SLANDEROUS LIE. The British Imperialist Campaign in Ireland is waged only to safeguard the fat profits of a few rich pigs and power crazy politicians.

We warn all unemployed brothers and sisters. Do not be fooled by the army recruiting campaign. An army career isn't fun in the sun and learning a useful trade, if you join you'll be trained in Belfast, Derry and all the other working class ghettos in Northern Ireland to murder and brutalise ordinary working class people. The training will come in useful when the boss class sends the troops into Clydeside, Merseyside, Tyneside, Birmingham, London and all the working class districts throughout Britain. To any unemployed worker thinking of joining up we ask you one question: WHICH WAY WILL YOU POINT YOUR GUN WHEN THE OFFICERS ORDER YOU AGAINST THE PEOPLE OF YOUR OWN TOWN?...Who will you shoot when your parents, brothers and sisters are in sight of your gun?

The British boss class has lined its pockets with the accumulated profits of 700 years of exploitation of the Irish working people. Now they are killing to defend these profits. THE ANGRY BRIGADE ADVISES THE BRITISH

RULING CLASS TO GET OUT OF IRELAND AND TAKE THEIR PUP-PETS (LYNCH, FAULKNER, ETC) WITH THEM. ANGRY BRIGADE. MOONLIGHTER'S CELL. POINT YOUR GUN.

AUGUST 18: Inspector Mould of the Fraud Squad gets a tip off from a snout that Anna Mendelson is living at 395 Amhurst Road. Mould duly calls through to Commander Bond with the news and the two meet that evening, along with Habershon, who's about to go on leave. Although Mendelson's only wanted for fraud at this stage, there are, as Bond puts it, other matters to consider. So he orders the house to be put under surveillance and waits. 'Get It On' by Stoke Newington's finest T. Rex is now No. 1.

AUGUST 19: John Barker and an unknown girl ('Rosemary Pink') go to Boulogne to meet Hilary Creek. Though Barker and Creek claim they meet by coincidence at Boulogne docks. There, according to the police, they split the consignment of gelignite so at least some of it will get through customs. But they all get aboard the 5.15 ferry to Dover unchecked and return to Amhurst Road at midnight, allegedly putting the gelignite in a cupboard under some clothes.

AUGUST 20: 9.00am: 2 Special Branch men in a blue Volkswagen begin the stakeout of 395 Amhurst Road from the church yard opposite.

10.00am: Jim Greenfield goes out to the phone box on the corner. The Special Branch men recognise him and call Mould at Scotland Yard. He instructs Bomb Squad Sergeant Gilham to get a stolen goods warrant and informs Bond that he's about to raid the house.

4.00pm: A squad of 8 prepare for the raid at Stoke Newington police station, just up the high street from Amhurst Road.

4.15pm: Sergeant Gilham and his squad burst into the top floor flat of 395 Amhurst Road, catching Barker, Creek, Greenfield and Mendelson unawares. Anna Mendelson then Jim Greenfield are duly arrested for fraud and bundled away to Albany Street (from where the original warrants had been issued). Then Sergeants Gilham and Davies allegedly find the gelignite, along with a sten gun under a table, the Beretta used in the 1967 US Embassy attack, detonators, the duplicator used to run off the 'Moonlighters Cell' communique and the Angry Brigade 'John Bull' printing set. According to the police, Barker and Creek tell them the stuff belongs to the Angry Brigade then burst out laughing. Hilary Creek subsequently attempts to escape through the kitchen window. Then Sergeants Gilham and Davies take Barker and Creek over the road to Stoke Newington nick. Gilham reports back to Bond and returns to the flat with Davies to 'make up his notes'.

5.45pm: Bond and Mould arrive at Amhurst Road to oversee proceedings. The guns and gelignite are laid out and photographed, then Bond orders everything to be taken to Albany Street. Including Barker and Creek.

7.45pm: Barker and Creek join Greenfield and Mendelson in the cells at Albany Street.

9.30pm: Explosives expert Captain Hawkins concludes his search of Amhurst Road and drives in convoy with the other officers and evidence to Albany Street. On his arrival everything is laid out in the charge room and the four are brought in to see it. According to the police, Jim Greenfield says, "Yes, fair enough" and Hilary Creek says, "Is that all you've woken me up for?" .

AUGUST 21: 12.00am: 2 officers go to Greenfield's cell with 2 batteries allegedly found with the guns. According to the police, Greenfield tells them that he brought the stuff back from Boulogne. But according to Greenfield, he's given a bit of a doing over, which involves being grabbed by the testicles and bounced from wall to wall by PC Ashenden. Barker claims he's dragged from his cell by his hair and held upside down with his head down a toilet, whilst simultaneously getting a kicking.

10.00am: After Commander Bond orders another series of raids and the continued surveillance of 395 Amhurst Road, Stuart Christie enters the house and goes up to the top floor. There he's met by one dozing copper and two more (from the church-yard) coming up the stairs behind him. Christie is duly searched and taken over the road to Stoke Newington nick, before joining the others at Albany Street. (At the time of the raid, Christie had been seeing press contacts about acting as inter-mediary in the Tupamaros kidnapping of the British Ambassador to Uruguay, Geoffrey Jackson, possibly getting Purdie and Prescott's release in to the bargain.

Jim Greenfield

He'd subsequently pranged the car he
shared with Albert Meltzer and was
angling to borrow some money off John
Barker to get it fixed.)
11.30am: Chris Bott calls round at
Amhurst Road for a drink with John
Barker and also finds himself in the
cells at Albany Street. According to the
police he says, "It's not my scene
what's going on there... You know what
I mean, dynamite."
12.30pm: Bond begins questioning Jim
Greenfield at Albany Street. According
to the police, Greenfield takes the rap
for the explosives, but denies any
knowledge of the guns (which were in a
holdall in his and Mendelson's room).
Barker doesn't say anything. Ditto
Stuart Christie, until he's shown the
contents of his car, which has been
impounded. Christie says some of the

Stuart Christie

car's contents belong to him, the rest to Albert Meltzer, who co-owns it. Then
Bond produces a box containing 2 detonators, which he claims were found in the
boot. Thereupon Christie says; "Those detonators weren't in the car and you know
it. I agree with all those, but not the detonators." Before the night is out, Bond also
interviews Mendelson and Creek, with similarly negative results.

Christie has a good anecdote about the police at Albany Street, when he's taken
to be interviewed by CID DS Davies;

*As we passed, Cremer gave me a shy smile in his inimitable manner, as if to say
simultaneously that he was sorry to see me there, that it was really nothing to do
with him, and he looked forward to many more pleasant chats. Davies looked at
him as he disappeared down the corridor. "Bloody Special Branch!" he said. I
breathed again. He sounded almost as though we had something in common - a
dislike of the political police.*

AUGUST 22: As the story hits the Sunday papers, Bond concludes his interviews
with Chris Bott, orders more raids (round Islington, Holloway, Stoke Newington,
Kilburn and Notting Hill), then decides to charge all 6 with conspiracy to cause
explosions.
AUGUST 23: The 6 arrested at Amhurst Road are charged at Albany Street with;

(i) Conspiring to cause explosions between January 1, 1968 and August 21, 1971.

(ii) Possessing explosive substances for an unlawful purpose.

(iii) Possessing a pistol without a firearms certificate.

(iv) Possessing 8 rounds of ammunition without firearms certificate.

(v) Possessing two machine guns without the authority of the Secretary of State.

(vi) Possessing 36 rounds of ammunition without firearms certificate.

(vii) Just Greenfield; attempting to cause an explosion in May 1970.

(viii) Greenfield/Mendelson; attempting to cause an explosion in Manchester in October 1970.

(ix) Christie; possessing one round of ammunition without firearms certificate; from 2 years previous.

(x) Barker/Greenfield/Christie; possessing explosive substances.

(xi) Barker/Greenfield/Creek; receiving stolen vehicle.

(xii) Christie; possessing explosive substances (the two detonators).

AUGUST 24: The six appear at Clerkenwell Magistrates' Court and Commander Bond reveals his true identity to oppose bail. Greenfield and Mendelson are also charged with conspiring with Bott, Purdie, Prescott, Wolf Seeberg, Martin Housden, Peter Truman, Christine Haisall, Rosemary Fiore (who my mate Barry used to go out with) and other persons unknown, 'to cheat and defraud such persons who could be induced to part with money and goods by the use of stolen cheque books, credit cards and identity documents and other fraudulent means and devices contrary to common law (between February 12 and May 11, 1971).' All six are remanded in custody and sent down, to Brixton and Holloway respectively, to await trial.

Following the detention of the six, Brixton and Holloway are subject to an influx of prison reform leaflets, which are at least partly responsible for an outbreak of prison occupations, demonstrations and riots. According to Stuart Christie a lot of younger prisoners get into Che Guevara and the Tupamaros; and Jim Greenfield becomes a bit of a hero on the inside when he persuades a fellow prisoner to plead innocent, against his lawyer's advice, thus assuring his acquittal.

SEPTEMBER 6: Habershon returns from holiday in France and sets to work, sifting through all the stuff seized at Amhurst Road. Fingerprints and handwriting samples are cross-referenced with evidence already in his files, and in due course Habershon gets a result. Fingerprints on a newspaper found with the unexploded Paddington Green bomb check out as Greenfield's. The fingerprint boys also come up with marks on a copy of 'Rolling Stone' linking Greenfield and Mendelson with the Manchester Italian Consulate bomb. 'Won't Get Fooled Again' by the Who drops out of the charts.

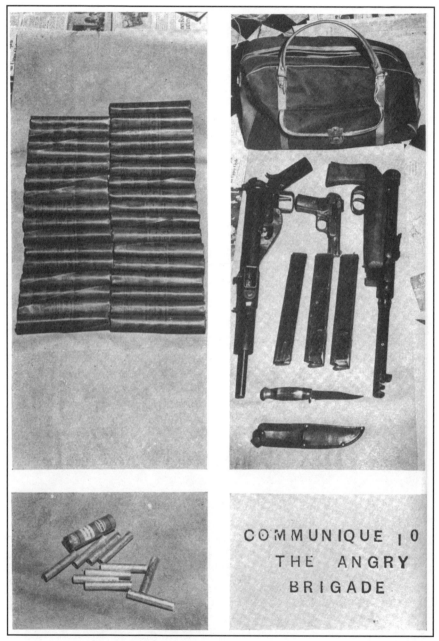

Interesting Arsenal found near Highbury in Arsenal's double winning year.

BRITISH JUSTICE

FRENDZ ANGRY BRIGADE SPECIAL - FREE IAN AND JAKE - A WORKING CLASS HERO IS SOMETHING TO BE - PANIC IN HIGH PLACES - COMMANDER X DECLARES WAR - CHRIS BRYANT AND THE GPO TOWER

SEPTEMBER 7: The original start date of the Purdie and Prescott trial: After the Amhurst Road arrests, the police apply to have everybody tried together but, because Purdie and Prescott have already been held for 6 months, the court decides to proceed with separate trials. Purdie and Prescott's trial date is now set for November 10.

SEPTEMBER 10: Ipswich Court is firebombed.

SEPTEMBER 16: An unexploded bomb is found in the officers' mess at Dartmoor Prison, and the 'Frendz' Angry Brigade special #10 (38) announces a march on Brixton Prison (before the trial date's changed);

THERE'S NO JUSTICE LIKE BRITISH JUSTICE: FREE IAN AND JAKE

It's another political trial, another attack on the alternative society and our life style. Don't kid yourself the trial only involves Ian and Jake - it's about the whole operation of the Special Branch - the special snoopers on our lives, employed by the state to suck information OUT OF the movement and INTO THEIR FILES. This is what the raids have been about. If a trial verdict was decided on evidence Ian and Jake could sit back in their cells in the certain knowledge of freedom by the end of September. But in a political trial evidence doesn't count for very much - the prejudices of the judge and jury more than compensate for the absurd lack of evidence. Remember the OZ trial, the case of the Little Red School Book, the Oval House riot (which the pigs caused and the Black Panthers were convicted of) - infact, when did a fair trial ever take place?

67

When Purdie and Prescott enter the courtroom they enter the sacred chambers of bigotry based on centuries of legal precedents. Every judge drinks and dines with the Special Branch - and he enjoys the camouflage of law to conceal the tyranny of the bench. No judges have neutral feelings about this case - you're on one side, or the Angry Side - and whether Ian and Jake ever actually threw a bloody bomb in their lives, is a secondary consideration. The paramount deciding factor is can Ian and Jake find a jury with at least 4 angry members - Angry jurors, angry about the fact that the secret police of this country can strut in and out of courtrooms, dragging off suspects just as they please, barge in on other court cases, pervert the course of justice... and GET AWAY WITH IT!

In the course of this case Moscow-gestapo tactics have happened here - one girl was even kicked and punched, and an old man intervened and threatened to call the police. The 3 assailants told him to 'fuck off' because 'WE ARE THE POLICE'. The pigs are the law-abiding thieves of our society - we all know corruption and bribery is part of the lawman's wage packet, Soho dealers in porno, the betting shop tycoons - senior detectives at the Yard take their cut, everyone knows that by any definition Scotland Yard is stacked full of criminals, and they're not all in cells - no siree. They're sittin' behind office desks and files.

We should not be surprised that in political cases - well-known agitators and friends are framed-up - for the pigs it's just part of the job. For the Special Branch there is no other way to fix undesirables - either jail them, deport them or both (like Paul Hoch). This case is a test-case for all our freedoms. It's YOU and ME, the people vs. the Thought Police. Never mind the 'conspiracy to cause explosions' charge - they know the real charges are the same the world over 'dangerous thoughts and anti-state activities'.

Ian & Jake are our moral consciences in the dock - millions share their beliefs and their anger - it could be any one of us facing a life-sentence for our way of life. For something we didn't do. Liberty is the enemy of the state, thus the civil liberties we talk so much about in Britain are the broken brittle threads of a liberalism that doesn't exist. We are not a permanent police-state like South Africa, yet we are permanently in danger of becoming one. The National Council for Civil Liberties is a bleating, protesting voice in the wilderness - no punch, no power; Reggie Maudling knows he can break any law he wants to if it helps him to preserve law and order - and to get 2 scapegoats for the Angry Brigade is top priority - show the people that resistance to repression doesn't pay.

When the law breaks the law there is no law. The police enter the Old Bailey on September 7th formally charged with false imprisonment of 4 girls, assault and wrongful arrest. The defence has to prove to the jury, that by their own liberal standards - the pigs are criminals, and the sort of criminals who injure the interests of the majority in society. Ian and Jake have already declared "We reject the role of being defendants, we are the accusers in this court." (Barnet commitals)

Ian and Jake and the movement can only win through our collective strength - in the court and outside - and through a bold exposé of the cynical truth - manipulations of the Special Branch.

This is a trial we have to win, brothers and sisters. We need your help to win it. SEE YOU AT CLAPHAM COMMON, 12 NOON, SATURDAY SEPTEMBER 4th. MARCH ON BRIXTON NICK - bring the subversive sunshine with you, let's conspire for fun and gaiety in the streets to fuck-up their conspiracy, let the inmates of Brixton know the alternative society can SHOUT and SCREAM, as often as THEY wield their axe of repression. ALL POWER TO THE CREEPING CRAWLING MEATBULL!!!

The 'Frendz' Angry Brigade special also includes an Angries chronology and the following articles;

ANGRY BRIGADE STRIKES/GOVERNMENT PANICS

In November last year Agitprop asked in their news-sheet, 'Red Notes', 'are there in fact urban guerrillas in England?' They continued, 'recently, two Londoners were charged with six counts of arson, including three against military establishments. More significant is that the police were trying to get information about 20 other such bombings that have taken place, including such targets as a Barclays Bank in the West End. Clearly things have been happening that haven't been reported... It is important to know that there are people engaged in concrete destruction. Publicity will come as the targets become increasingly more central and important to the power structure of the enemy.'

PANIC IN HIGH PLACES/COMMANDER X DECLARES WAR

There was a time when the British people could be trusted by the government to work hard for their masters, long hours without complaint for that noble cause... the national interest. But nowadays Robert Carr can't even finish his cornflakes before the morning papers batter him with the news of yet another strike (Oh no! Not Fords again). Sign upon sign of the flagging loyalties of the British worker. And then strikes took a vicious turn for the worse - outright political strikes against Robert Carr's gift to British management, the Industrial Relations Bill, a magnificent effort on the part of the Employment Minister to live up to his reputation as the former big chief of Securicor. This lack of patriotism has been getting on some people's nerves - particularly the bosses, bankers and Robert Carrs. And then our frightened rulers suffered something like shellshock at the news of Robert Carr's kitchen falling apart, as a result of one of the Angry Brigade's rare public appearances in Hadley Green, Barnet.

This report of the shelling of Carr's home, sent ministers of the crown scurrying down the corridors of power for summit talks with security chiefs. Later, it is understood from a government spokesman, that several ministers visited their psychiatrist, who made every attempt to con members of the government that ordinary people really like them and really don't want to throw bombs at them, and that all this talk of people getting angry with the government was just a question of childhood fears of inadequacy.

Several days after January 12th, ministers returned to work and orders went out to the Barnet bomb squad and Special Branch to look for likely candidates to qualify for the privileges of a state invitation to appear at Barnet Magistrates Court charged with assorted outrages and anarchist leanings.

Sure enough a likely candidate soon emerged, and the press reported that Chief Supt. Blundershon and his 500 men were hot on the trail of a notorious Glaswegian Anarchist known for his exploits in Spain, and impeccable Scotland Yard sources of information assured us that ports and airports all over were being checked for this number one suspect.

However, misfortune struck. The star candidate for the Carr bombings, far from being an international fugitive chased from country to country by the bloodhounds of Interpol, turned out to have been quietly vegetating at work throughout the period, and that Special Branch although making a host of enquiries with his workmates, never quite got round to interviewing the man himself. The whole story was, according to Special Branch sources, a bit of a red-herring. (Since then the red-herring has finally been arrested - Christie the man they've suspected of every bombing in the last ten years.) Thus thwarted in the search for an immediate arrest, Blundershon and co. turned their attentions to the other 4,670,238 persons known (according to Special Branch files) to have strong views in opposition to the Industrial Relations Bill. Blundershon and Special Branch put two and two together, and declared that members of the Angry Brigade were to be found among 4 million opponents of the bill. And then a turning point in the investigations came when another clue emerged. The suspects were probably to be counted amongst the 7 1/2 million sisters and supporters of Women's Liberation because phantom bombers claimed to have blown up a TV van at the Miss World Contest.

As there were rather a lot of suspects, Chief Supt. Blundershon told the magistrates I need rather a lot of search warrants for explosives and the Barnet gang became regular guests at the homes of rather a lot of left-wing sympathisers. Special Branch even made guest appearances at Bow St. Magistrates Court on Feb. 11th, and Chief Supt. Blundershon did a routine round-up of candidates, and four girls who were under the impression that they were going to be witnesses in the Women's Liberation trial, found themselves the reluctant recipients of the hospitality of Barnet police station (the fare is not recommended even though the coffee is free).

With entry qualifications being so low, and the number of telephones being tapped so high, and our brave rulers demanding results in such a hurry, (Ted Heath gave orders to Bumbleshon "Get those responsible and all those who associate with them, and turn London over, if you have to") that it comes as no surprise when Chief Supt. Bumbleshon announced that a Mr Jake Prescott had got the job - scapegoat of the year for the Carr bombings. Prescott, first man in, was soon to be joined by 'Mr obvious candidate Purdie' (Purdie was so close to Prescott over the last four months that they even spent some time in the same cell together - a 'very obvious candidate' for the outrage) who was arrested owing to a confusion between explosives and his person...

And so we must conclude that the case against Purdie is that Ian Purdie is an explosive substance, that when ignited is likely to explode, and that he should be handled with extreme care. Judge X, please take careful note!

The plot thickened, the conspiracy grew, Dorian Williams for the prosecution up at Barnet committals held the court spellbound on the first day with tales of anarchist intrigue and hushed conversations in hippy communes where strangers would be asked to leave the magic circle of conspirators. Sinister organisations have been named like Claimants Unions, which include a new unknown quantity in terrorist circles, the clubbing together of embittered angry old age pensioners. Their anger about their social security payments is all too familiar to those staunch servants of the state, social security officers who sit patiently behind their counters fending off the angry brigade of old age pensioners, who will stop at nothing to get their giros. The secret service are clearly not fooled by all that stuff about legal rights and these people being too old to mess about with bombs. The clear unadulterated evidence is that Claimant Unions are stuffed full of angry people just like Women's Liberation, People's Association, Ford workers, Post Office workers and all the rest.

Obviously, the state is playing it cool and not revealing the full extent of the conspiracy - this is why mystery man Commander X's name was kept secret - for reasons in the national interest. The public might easily be shocked into a state of panic at the size and extent of this conspiracy - your next-door neighbour might be involved.

Is your wife angry? Is your milkman against the Industrial Relations Bill? Is your daughter for womens' liberation? Does your husband show violent tendencies after he comes home refreshed from a day's soul-fulfilling machine minding? Is the person sitting next to you on the tube a member of the Angry Brigade?

Scotland Yard hasn't yet confirmed how widespread the danger is, but it's clear the prosecution in the Carr bombing case are hiding something from the public at large. They are afraid to reveal how much they know in case of general alarm. Is this why they didn't mention the other angry brigade bombings at Fords and Bibas. But, no matter how afraid our rulers are, no matter how much they are

71

holding back information in our own interests, surely we have the right to know?

We demand the Special Branch tell us, and tell us now, whether it's not just other people, but that it's you and me, we want to know, are we members of the Angry Brigade?

WHO'S WHO IN THE ANGRY BRIGADE

Commander X is Ernest R. Bond: formerly one of Challenor's chums at West End Central, then promoted for services rendered to the state to CS department of Scotland Yard (CID complaints section - important for public relations & the good image of the British cop). No one knows how Ernest got this job; he is known as Mr 'rough and ready' Commander X, and this is most certainly the major reason for his appointment. Has very low opinion of Habershon, and kept him well clear of the recent top-secret, super-commander X operation, resulting in 6 arrests.

Chief Superintendent Roy Habershon: fall-guy and front-man for the hunt for the elusive 'Angry Brigade'. Blundershon's tactics produced no results except for the Ian & Jake frame-up, all his friends at the Yard told him to cool it - bit of a joke in intelligence circles; played no part in the Amhurst Road operation. Doesn't have many friends left, so spends a lot of time going through left-wing address books trying to meet new ones - Habershon's 'Thoughts on Anarchism' coming out soon; probably won't be a best seller. Can't make up his mind whether Ian Purdie is an anarchist or not - Habershon used to be in charge of Upper Street Islington police station (1969) which is perhaps why he can't resist raiding pads in Islington.

Chief Superintendent Curtis - Special Branch: this member of the thought police starred in the March 19 raid on a house in Talbot Road - and used his pig head to scan the Powis Square trial defence documents, which the Special Branch found 'interesting reading'.

Detective Chief Superintendent Dixon (not of Dock Green): regular companion on Habershon's raids, his hobbies include reading love letters and address books.

Detective Inspector Barlow: straight off 'Z Cars' onto the real thing, Barlow is very touchy about the Stephen McCarthy case and is rather lacking in the finer arts of interrogation. Block-headed right-wing sort, and can't even begin to conceal it. Doesn't get on with Curtis and Dixon and the Special Branch.

Detective Inspector Mould: obsessed with using explosives warrants as an excuse for cheque spotting (ie. Can't keep his hands off cheque-books). Easy to recognise - Hitler type moustache which twitches like a music hall imitation of the Fuhrer.

Affectionately known as Adolf to his friend. His fraud-squad connections don't inhibit our friend Mould from attending demos - rumoured to have good Special Branch connections.

Detective Sergeant Creamer - Special Branch: prides himself on being Special Branch expert on political groupings - favourite questions include: "Are you an anarcho-syndicalist or an international situationist?" Owing to his obvious grasp of a few minor details, Creamer has failed to get promotion on the grounds that 'he is too clever by half', with his university education and all. Well read but too intellectual - not popular with CID regulars like Habershon and Barlow.

Detective Constable Robson - Special Branch: always in action, always asking questions, never gets anywhere.

Max the Labrador dog who never finds explosives: employed by the state to sniff out explosives, very reliable and friendly, never finds anything, and takes more interest in nourishing marrow-bone jelly. Definitely the most human member of their regular raiding parties.

A GELLY PARTY AT STOKE NEWINGTON

Two weeks ago Commander X - known to his friends as Commander Ernest Bond of the Yard - master-minded operation gelly-party. This resulted in 5 raids on London flats (put out by ever-reliable Scotland Yard as 20 raids) - and finally bumping into some real live gelignite and ammunition, busting 6 brothers and sisters in the process. Scotland Yard emphatically denies the suggestion that these explosives found at Amhurst Road, Stoke Newington, were planted. Surprise, surprise Stuart Christie, the 'mad bomber' of Spain - the man they were dying to get - was among those arrested, for just being in the same street.

So after 9 months of Angry Brigade in action against the state, 6 months of Blundershoning (Habershon) investigations, all we know is that some explosives and jelly-babies have finally been found. We know nothing more. Were the four people found living with the gelly - some part of some Angry Brigade? Of course the police say - of course, it's THEM! Well 'Frendz' will wait for the next revolutionary bombing of the ruling class, before we make up our minds about those just arrested. One thing's certain - Ian and Jake are innocent in all senses - they have been framed - and no effort should be spared to prove it. Frame-ups are one of the much-under-estimated features of British justice - but beware, the scriptwriting talents of the Special Branch should not be lightly disregarded. Not many juries are clued-up on the finer points of legal conspiracies against enemies of the state. By Jelly Baby.

SEPTEMBER 20: Another wave of bomb attacks begin with one under Chelsea Bridge, opposite the army barracks. The blast is heard 3 miles away.

SEPTEMBER 24: Albany Street Army Barracks is next, just down the road from the Bomb Squad headquarters. Getting closer...

LATE SEPTEMBER: 'Fireball' by Deep Purple replaces 'Who's Next' at the top of the album chart and the Stones release 'Gimme Shelter'.

OCTOBER 15: Maryhill Army Barracks in Glasgow are firebombed.

OCTOBER 20: The home of Christopher Bryant, a Birmingham building contractor, is bombed during a strike and claimed for the Angry Brigade by another communique;

The Angry Brigade bombing of Chris Bryant's home in Birmingham has brought attention to the activities of the Bryant building combine. For two weeks workers on a Bryant site have been on strike demanding a flat rate of one pound an hour and the end of 'the Lump' - a pool of self-employed non-union men available for hire. The blast badly damaged the front of Bryant's six bedroomed house but as with other AB bombings, didn't hurt anyone.

Capitalism is a vicious circle. People's sweat and blood is used and exploited. They make us produce shit... they give us next to nothing while their class pockets huge profits... the ruling class... the Bryants of this world. Then, when we put the overalls aside, we clean the muck from our faces and we take the boring bus or train home and they suddenly transform us into consumers. In other words when we are not working they make us buy... the same shit we produced. The miserable wage packet they gave us they make us spend on useless food, on machines specially designed to break down and on houses we know look and feel like prisons.

Prisons we helped build. And paid (more specifically promised to pay over the next twenty years for we never have enough dough to pay for a house or a car or anything for that matter - they have to exploit us even more by making us pay interest) for them. We build the prisons and then we live in them. We produce shit and then we eat it. Producers of shit - consumers of shit.

There are many of our brothers and sisters inside. An old revolutionary once called prisons 'an occupational hazard'. A hazard which may hit any person who chooses to take a action. But to lose a finger, a limb, your lungs - any accident at work - this too is an occupational hazard. Look at the safety precautions on Bryant's sites - none at all. Not only a limb but your life. So what's the bloody difference?

Chris Bryant made £1,714,857 profit last year - a 25 per cent rise on 1969. He does it by a cocktail of high society, high finance and a lot of corruption. He has clinched his deals for the redevelopment of Birmingham on the golf courses of Solihull with Corporation Councillors. The Councillors oblige by

charging high rents on the Council estates - like Chelmsley Wood - to pay high prices to Bryant for his contracts. Now he's buying up land around Solihull to sell to the same Council who will give him the contracts to develop it, with our money. No one should be conned that the Birmingham Mail is anything other than the Bryant broadsheet either. A man who lives in a mock Tudor village ('Windways', Jacobean Road, Knowle) doesn't have to worry about the next HP instalment, doesn't have to nick a can of paint from work to make his house look decent, doesn't have to worry about draughts. (But today... did we say Windways?) We'll hit million for million... We'll follow him from Tudor village to Tudor village.

25 years we've waited in Birmingham for a building strike. Bryant hit us and bullied us with the lump. By hitting Bryant we're hitting the lump too. The Woodgate Valley stands for class solidarity and Revolution. The Workers have taken their stand. Sabotage in the place of work is a reality. The bosses are beginning to feel the undiluted power of the people. The people are hitting back.

The Brigade is hitting back. Now we are too many to know each other. Yet we recognise all those charged with crimes against property as our brothers and sisters. The Stoke Newington 6, the political prisoners in Northern Ireland are all prisoners of the class war.

We are not in a position to say whether any one person is or isn't a member of the Brigade. All we say is: the Brigade is everywhere.

Without any Central Committee and no hierarchy to classify our members, we can only know strange faces as friends through their actions. We love them, we embrace them as we know others will. Other cells, sections, groups.

LET TEN MEN AND WOMEN MEET WHO ARE RESOLVED ON THE LIGHTNING OF VIOLENCE RATHER THAN THE LONG AGONY OF SURVIVAL; FROM THIS MOMENT DESPAIR ENDS AND TACTICS BEGIN. POWER TO THE PEOPLE. THE BRIGADE IS ANGRY.

(NB. 'From this moment despair ends and tactics begins' is one of Raoul Vaneigem's.)

OCTOBER 31: 4.30am: The viewing gallery on the 31st floor of the GPO (Telecom) Tower is devastated by another Angry Brigade bomb. As is 'The Cunning Man' pub in Reading, where M4 workers have been refused service. The GPO Tower is promptly closed to the public, though the revolving Top of the Tower restaurant survives the blast and opens again for business 6 weeks later. No one ever claims responsibility for this attack but in the fictionalised novel 'The Angry Brigade', by the barrister Alan Burns, there's a suspect account of the planting of the bomb, where the cowardly leader 'Ivor' gets his girlfriend

'Suzanne' to go up the tower with the bomb, while her gay accomplice 'Barry' also chickens out. John Lennon's 'Imagine' is now top of the album chart.

NOVEMBER 1: Another bomb attack on the Army Tank HQ in Everton Street.

NOVEMBER 6: Bomb attacks on Lloyds Bank in Amsterdam, the Italian Consulate in Basle and British Embassies in Rome and Barcelona. Another joint effort in support of the 'Stoke Newington 6' and Italian anarchists in a similar position. While in West Germany the RAF are still robbing banks and starting to kill coppers.

The GPO (Telecom) Tower after
Angries bombing. Still remains
closed to the public to this day .

PURDIE AND PRESCOTT

MR A AND MR B - MORE ARRESTS - 15 YEARS FOR ADDRESSING 3 ENVELOPES - WE ARE ALL ANGRY - THE STOKE NEWINGTON SIX/SEVEN/EIGHT/NINE/TEN

NOVEMBER 10: The trial of Purdie and Prescott finally begins. They are charged with conspiring 'unlawfully and maliciously to cause explosions likely to endanger life or cause serious injury to property,' with Barker, Bott, Christie, Creek, Greenfield and Mendelson, between July 30, 1970 and March 7, 1971. Prescott is also charged with personally carrying out the bomb attacks on Robert Carr and the DEP. The evidence against Prescott mainly consists of what his cellmates at Brixton, Mr A and B, say he told them about his involvement in the Angry Brigade; cross-linked with addresses and lists found at Amhurst Road. Then there's his handwriting/fingerprints on the Carr communique envelopes, and the evidence of the 2 girls from Edinburgh, who say how revolutionary Prescott got after he met Purdie. And that's about the extent of the prosecution case against Purdie. His counsel, a Mr Shindler, instructs Purdie not to bother to take the stand in his own defence. 'Maggie May' by Rod Stewart and the Faces is No. 1.

NOVEMBER 11: Another name is added to the indictment list when Angela Weir is arrested after a raid on Haverstock Street, Islington. She's taken to Albany Street, where Habershon accuses her of being Barker's companion on the Boulogne trip. Before charging her with conspiracy to cause explosions, making it the 'Stoke Newington 7'.

NOVEMBER 17: 89 Talbot Road is raided again and Chris Allen, who works as a play worker with Notting Hill People's Association, is arrested and charged with conspiracy to cause explosions; making it 8.

NOVEMBER 26: Pauline Conroy, a university lecturer and West London's Claimants Union founder, is arrested round the corner on Powis Square and similarly charged, making it 9. Her and Chris Allen are both subsequently shipped over to Albany Street for questioning.

NOVEMBER 29: Broadstairs Courthouse is firebombed.

DECEMBER 1: The Purdie and Prescott trial comes to a conclusion after 3 weeks. Ian Purdie is acquitted on all charges but Jake Prescott is found guilty of conspiracy to cause explosions. Even though it can't be proved that he had anything to do with the Carr and DEP bombings. He effectively gets 15 years for addressing 3 envelopes. In his summing up the judge, Justice Melford Stevenson again, concedes;

"I do not doubt that you were chosen as a tool by people more sinister than you are, and I suspect more intelligent. They are as yet unidentified, but I must equally face the fact that you knowingly embraced the conspiracy... the most evil conspiracy I have ever had to deal with."

(Prior to Purdie and Prescott, Stevenson presided over the Krays trial - Incidentally, Jack 'The Hat' McVitie gets his in 1967 round the corner from 395 Amhurst Road, on Evering Road, where Sid Vicious is living in 1974, when he's first arrested for assaulting 2 coppers and subsequently smashing a window in Stoke Newington police station.)

Despite his acquittal, Purdie goes back to prison to await trial for the cheque fraud, but he is eventually granted bail.
DECEMBER 2: 'The Guardian' condemns Prescott's sentence as 'exceedingly severe' and the whole trial as 'an unsatisfactory affair.'
DECEMBER 4: West Berlin police kill suspected terrorist Georg von Rauch.
DECEMBER 10: 'Time Out' adds to the condemnation of the Prescott verdict;

The phrase 'Now we are all angry' sums up the reaction of all radicals and revolutionaries. For unlike the 'Oz' trial, there is no middle ground. No liberal indignation.

While the newly formed Stoke Newington 8 Defence Group declares;

Every second of their lives; every time they feel great, every time they run and laugh and fuck together; they are part of the movement when they work with other revolutionaries doing countless other things. Being part of their revolution they are sensitive to the needs and desires of the revolution. On 12 January 1971 we had a one-day strike, we went on huge marches all over the country, we planned strategies for the future and we bombed Robert Carr.

DECEMBER 15: Attempted car ambush assassination of Zaid Rifai, the Jordanian Ambassador to London by Black September.
DECEMBER 16: 'it' #119 reports on the Purdie and Prescott trial;

THE BODY POLITIK

For addressing 3 envelopes, Jake Prescott was found guilty of conspiracy to bomb and sentenced to 15 years jail - 5 years for each envelope!
THE CHARGES . 1. That Jake Prescott and Ian Purdie conspired with Creek, Mendelson, Bott, Barker, Christie, Greenfield and persons unknown to cause explosions. 2. That Jake caused the explosion at the Dept. of Productivity in St. James's Square. 3. That Jake caused the explosion at Carr's house.
THE VERDICTS . Jake - not guilty of DEP bombing and Carr bombing - guilty of conspiracy. Ian - not guilty. THE SENTENCES. Jake - 15 years. Ian - still detained on cheques charges.
WE CHARGE that Justice Melford Stevenson, notorious Judge in the Cambridge Garden House Riot trial, was blatantly biased in his summing up and directions to the jury. That he failed to give a balanced summary of the evidence and that he continually emphasised the prosecution case and put down the defence. This is what he said:
CONSPIRACY. Stevenson's definition of conspiracy was important in its implications for future trials. He said it was 'an agreement to achieve an unlawful purpose... proof of an agreement is always a difficult matter... conspiracies are hatched in whispers... it is, or nearly always is, a matter of inference.' In other words, circumstantial proof will do. 'Likely candidates' (to use Supt. Habershon's words) are all the pigs need to find.
THE POLITICS. 'In one sense, politics here don't matter... there is only one sense in which politics acquire any relevance in this case. That is so far as you see they may provide evidence of a motive for what is alleged to be done here.' In other words, politics matter where the pigs want them to.
THE STOKE NEWINGTON SIX. Much of the prosecution case dealt with the 'arsenal' found in the raid on Amhurst Road and with Jake and Ian's connections with the Stoke Newington 6. Stevenson dwelt on these details and accepted the prosecution 'proof' that the 6 were guilty, despite the fact that the 6 have not yet been tried and had no charge to answer.
THE EVIDENCE AGAINST JAKE. Briefly, it was Jake's visit to Edinburgh (supposedly to steal explosives), Methven and Steer's experience of staying with Jake in London, the handwriting on Angry Brigade envelopes, the evidence of Mr. A and Mr. B - ex. cell-mates of Jake, who said he had described bombing Carr's house. Stevenson presented to the jury the stark choice that either there was a 'wicked conspiracy' between A, B and Habershon or Jake's alibi witnesses were to be believed. And there was, he said, 'Nothing easier in the world than to set up a false alibi, which the prosecution have no chance of testing'.
THE EVIDENCE AGAINST IAN. Basically, said Stevenson, Ian knew 5 of the Stoke Newington 6. He had written letters 'allying himself with Prescott'. So des-

perate was Stevenson's attempt to implicate Ian that he even quoted an Angry Brigade communique saying, 'Solidarity, Revolution & Love' and compared it with a letter to Jake signed 'Love, Solidarity, Revolution'. Talking about Ian's interview with Habershon, Stevenson said 'Purdie replied time after time with the words 'No Comment'... or some far from courteous answer.' (!) Referring to Ian's decision not to present a defence, Stevenson said sarcastically, 'Purdie has chosen not to answer or explain any of the evidence... from which the Crown say it is impossible to avoid the inference that he made himself a party to the conspiracy'.

THE VERDICT. Surprisingly, despite Stevenson's gross attempt to mislead them, the jury was able to feel 'reasonable doubt' in Ian's case and on the 2 specific bomb charges against Jake. In throwing out the Carr bombing charge, the jury indicated they did not believe Mr. A and Mr. B and presumably, therefore, that they felt there was 'a wicked conspiracy' between A, B and Habershon (to quote Stevenson). The jury were deceived enough however to feel that Jake's admission that he wrote 3 Angry Brigade envelopes made him guilty of conspiracy.

THE SENTENCES. Stevenson used the jury's half-hearted verdict as an opportunity to give Jake a savage 15 years for his 'evil conspiracy'. He also gave Jake 5 years for cheques fraud charges to run concurrently. Ian's defence counsel applied for bail on the cheques charge but Habershon pointed out sinisterly, 'He has friends all over the world'. So Stevenson obligingly refused bail - despite the fact that all the other people in the cheques case have been granted it.

THE FUTURE. Application for Ian's bail will not now be possible until after the Stoke Newington 6's committal proceedings. He will then have been in prison for a year. The cheques case will not happen until after the trial of the 6, at the Old Bailey. September is thought to be the earliest likely date. Jake is appealing.

SOME QUESTIONS. Jake admitted writing envelopes containing communiques after the Carr bombing, but denied knowing what they were to be used for. Handwriting on every other Angry Brigade envelope was unidentifiable, so, if Jake knew what he was doing, why didn't he take similar precautions? After all the evidence and assumptions about them presented in this trial, how can the Stoke Newington 6 hope to get a 'fair trial'? Will there be an investigation into Habershon's 'wicked conspiracy' with A and B?

BETRAYED BY THE LAWYERS. It was the defence lawyers who accepted without a murmur on the first day of the trial an amendment to the charge of conspiracy to include the names of the Stoke Newington 6. This meant that the prosecution was able to, and did, drag up details of all 27 'outrages' at every opportunity. This enabled the prosecution to suggest, 'Therefore, if you find that the evidence is overwhelming, that those 6 persons arrested in August were some of the persons responsible anyway for those bombings, then it becomes important, does it not, to see what, if any, connection those 2 defendants had with any one or more of those 6 persons while they were at liberty over the period of the alleged conspiracy.'

WE ARE ALL ANGRY. Jake's sentence contrasts grossly with the 2 or 3 year sentence given to 2 youths for fire-bombing a West Indian party, which caused permanent injury to at least 10 black people. 'Justice' Stevenson's summing up and sentencing couldn't have been a better example of why people are angry and disillusioned with this society. But at the same time the straight media coverage of the Angry Brigade and the Jake and Ian trial has shown just how easily distorted righteous anger can be. Because the press on the subject read like an extension of Scotland Yard, people without personal contact with Angry Brigade sympathisers were only alienated from the bombings. The Brigade's reasoned reactions to a violent society became, in the media coverage, acts of senseless violence.

This may be why the spectacular bombings of the Angries have not really caught on so far in Britain. Although violence may well in the end be necessary to overthrow this repressive society and we all sympathise with the Angry Brigade, recent events suggest such actions should have a lot more popular support before they're attempted. The necessary working together with people and turning each other on cannot be cut short. Spectacular actions might be better if restricted to things that clearly ridicule and discredit this society and its leaders.

DECEMBER 18: Kate McLean, an art student, who's also suspected of being Barker's companion on the Boulogne trip, is arrested, making it the 'Stoke Newington 10'. She's charged, along with Angela Weir, Chris Allen and Pauline Conroy, with conspiring to cause explosions with the original 6. As 'Electric Warrior' by T. Rex becomes the No. 1 Xmas album and 'Meaty, Beaty, Big and Bouncy' by the Who enters the charts, the Xmas issue of 'it'(#120) looks back on 1971 as 'The Year of the Angry Brigade';

HERE COME DE JUDGE

In 1971, the government decided to fight the revolution in the courts. Using vague blanket charges, like conspiracy, they mounted 3 major trials - against Oz for obscenity, against Jake and Ian for bombing, and against the Mangrove for riot. In all 3 cases, the judge was blatantly biased, and in all 3 cases the jury saw through the lies and prejudice of judge and prosecution and threw charges out. The Oz men were found not guilty of conspiracy to corrupt minors, Ian Purdie not guilty of conspiracy to bomb and Jake Prescott not guilty to specific bombings, the Mangrove 9 not guilty of conspiracy to cause riot and affray...

1971 was also the year of the Angry Brigade. They first became widely known on 13 January, after a bomb exploded at the house of Robert Carr, Minister of Employment and the man responsible for the Industrial Relations Act. The AB would have forcefully expressed the anger and frustration of revolutionaries, if they had managed to relate more to a particular movement, be they freaks, work-

ers or what. As it was, they tended to seem isolated and while support for them was extensive, it was largely passive.

The Special Branch Bomb Squad, under Commander Bond, was active through-out the year and in the end ripped off a dozen good people from the community, while abusing our privacy and their own laws. In April, they found 2 likely candidates in Jake and Ian and kept them in jail for the rest of 1971. As their trial progressed, the bombings continued, and by October, even after the arrest of 6 people in Stoke Newington, the communiques were still coming, by now signed 'The Brigade is Angry'. Other groups evoked Angry Brigade name to campaign against obscenity laws, exploitation of kids and honky businessmen's ripoffs. 'We must attack. We cannot delegate our desire to take the offensive. Sabotage is reality... getting out of the factory is not the only way to strike... stay in and take over... we are against any external structure.' Communique 7. The Angry Brigade (March).

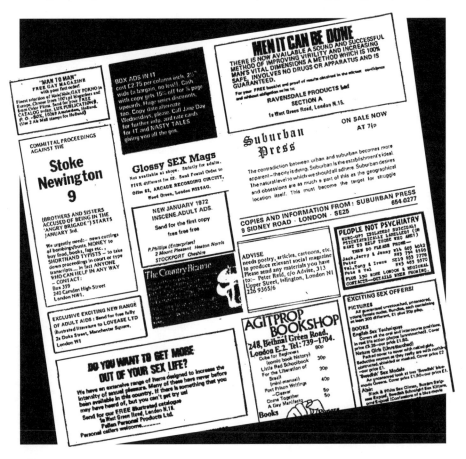

THE STOKE NEWINGTON EIGHT

1972: A CLOCKWORK ORANGE - COMMITTAL PROCEEDINGS AND CHARGES - STOKE NEWINGTON: TWO'S COMPANY, THREE'S A CONSPIRACY - BLOODY SUNDAY

JANUARY 1972: As 'A Clockwork Orange' opens in the West End and proto-Sex Pistols form in Shepherd's Bush, Attorney General Sir Peter Rawlinson (the victim of an early Angry Brigade attack) decides there's insufficient evidence to grant 'fiat' for a case against Chris Allen and Pauline Conroy. So they're released (with £100/£150 costs) and it's the 'Stoke Newington 8'. 'I'd Like to Teach the World to Sing' by the New Seekers is No. 1.

JANUARY 3: Committal proceedings against 'the 8' begin at Lambeth Magistrates Court. 'it' #121 reports on the proceedings;

ANGRY BRIGADE: MORE VICTORIES

Committal proceedings against the Stoke Newington 10 started with two more of the Angry Brigade 'conspirators' being freed. Pauline Conroy and Chris Allen were released last week after the Attorney-General announced he was not granting consent for proceedings to continue against them 'at this stage'. The phrase 'at this stage' was emphasised. Chris has been in jail since 18 November and Pauline had been on £20,200 bail.

Lord Gifford, asking for an order preventing police 'harassment' of Pauline, was told by a magistrate, Harold Beaumont, that his application was 'thoroughly ill-conceived'. The release of Pauline and Chris follows the 'not guilty' verdict on Ian Purdie at the Old Bailey. Ian has now been given bail on his cheque fraud charges on condition that he lives with his mother and reports to the pig station twice a day.

The hearing continues against Jim Greenfield, Anna Mendelson, Hilary Creek, Stuart Christie, Chris Bott, Angela Weir and Kate McLean, accused of 'conspiring together with Jake Prescott and others unknown between 1 January 1968 and 20 August 1971 to cause explosions likely to endanger life or cause serious injury to property'.

JANUARY 22: Another letter-bomb is sent to an MP at the House of Commons. JANUARY 24: The hearing at Lambeth ends after 3 weeks, and the 8 are committed for trial at the Old Bailey. The charge sheet now reads;

Regina v. James GREENFIELD, Anna MENDELSON, George BUCHANAN, alias John BARKER, Hilary Anne CREEK, James Stuart CHRISTIE, Christopher Michael G. BOTT, Angela Margaret WEIR, Catherine Judith McLEAN. For that they on diverse days between January 1, 1968, and August 20, 1971, in the Greater London Area and elsewhere, unlawfully and maliciously conspired together with Jack PRESCOTT and with persons unknown to cause by explosive substances explosions in the United Kingdom of a nature likely to endanger life or cause serious injury to property. Contrary to Section 3 (a) Explosive Substances Act, 1883.

James GREENFIELD and Anna MENDELSON. On or about October 9, 1970, at 26 Brown Street in the City of Manchester, unlawfully and maliciously attempted to cause by explosive substances an explosion in the United Kingdom of a nature likely to endanger life or to cause serious injury to property. Contrary to Section 3 (a) Explosive Substances Act, 1883.

Christopher BOTT, John BARKER, James GREENFIELD, James CHRISTIE, Hilary CREEK and Anna MENDELSON. On or about August 20, 1971, at 359 Amhurst Road, London N16, knowingly had in their possession or under their control certain explosive substances, namely, 33 3.5 oz. cartridges of explosive; 11 detonators; 1 cardboard box lid containing a plastic container with 6 Jetex charges therein; a tinplate lid; an electrical light switch cover and screw; 2 lengths of conductor wire; 1 length of lay flat flex; 1 2.5v. bulb; 1 1.5v. dry battery; 1 used tube of Bostik adhesive; 3 resistance panels; 1 piece of emery cloth; 1 pin; 1 polythene bag containing 1 length of nichrome wire; 1 length of white cotton string; 1 resistance element; 1 ruler scale; 2 PP3 9v. batteries connected in series; 1 part-used tube of Bostik adhesive; 1 pair of black leather gloves; 1 pair of black fabric gloves; one blue/grey holdall: in such circumstances as to give rise to a reasonable suspicion that they did not have them in their possession or under their control for a lawful object. Contrary to Section 4 (1) Explosive Substances Act, 1883.

85

John BARKER, James GREENFIELD and Hilary CREEK. On ór about August 20, 1971, at Walford Road, London N16, knowingly had in their possession or under their control certain explosive substances, namely a roll of 1/2" black insulating tape and a pair of scissors, in such circumstances as to give rise to a reasonable suspicion that they did not have them in their possession or under their control for a lawful object. Contrary to Section 4 (1) Explosive Substances Act, 1883.

James CHRISTIE. On or about August 20, 1971, at Sydner Road, London N16, knowingly had in his possession or under his control certain explosive substances, namely, 2 detonators and a screwdriver, in such circumstances as to give rise to a reasonable suspicion that he did not have them in his possession or under his control for a lawful object. Contrary to Section 4 (1) Explosive Substances Act, 1883.

James CHRISTIE. On or about June 10, 1970, at 16 Fonthill Road, Finsbury Park, London N4, had in his possession a round of 7.65mm ammunition without holding a Firearms Certificate in force at the time. Contrary to Section 1 (1) Firearms Act, 1968.

James GREENFIELD, John BARKER and Hilary CREEK. Between July 8, 1971 and August 20, 1971, in the Greater London Area, dishonestly handled a Hillman Avenger motor car, FGJ505J, knowing or believing the same to have been stolen. Contrary to Section 22 (1) Theft Act, 1968.

Christopher BOTT, John BARKER, James GREENFIELD, James CHRISTIE, Hilary CREEK and Anna MENDELSON. On or about August 20, 1971, at 359 Amhurst Road, London N16, had in their possession a Browning 7.65mm pistol without holding a Firearms Certificate in force at the time. Contrary to Section 1 (1) Firearms Act, 1968.

Christopher BOTT, John BARKER, James CHRISTIE, James GREEN-FIELD, Hilary CREEK and Anna MENDELSON. On or about August 20, 1971, at 359 Amhurst Road, London N16, had in their possession 81 rounds of ammunition without holding a Firearms Certificate in force at the time. Contrary to Section 1 (1) (b) Firearms Act, 1968.

Christopher BOTT, John BARKER, James GREENFIELD, James CHRISTIE, Hilary CREEK and Anna MENDELSON. On or about August 20, 1971, at 359 Amhurst Road, London N16, had in their possession without the authority of the Secretary of State, prohibited weapons, namely a Sten gun, a sub-machine gun and a Beretta sub-machine gun. Contrary to Section 5 (1) (a) Firearms Act, 1968.

James GREENFIELD. On or before May 22, 1970, at Harrow Road, London W2, unlawfully and maliciously attempted to cause by explosive substances an explosion in the United Kingdom of a nature likely to endanger life or cause serious injury to property. Contrary to Section 3 (a) Explosive Substances Act, 1883.

After the charges are read out John Barker replies with a statement, saying it won't be a fair trial because their guilt has already been assumed in the Purdie and Prescott trial and reported as such in the press. Barker goes on to accuse Habershon and Bond of conspiring to get a conviction by any means necessary and with interfering with defence preparations.

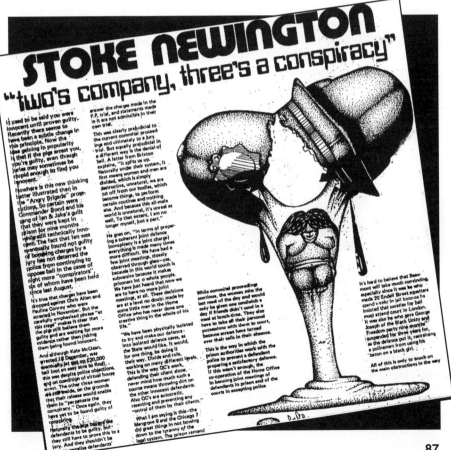

A N A R C H Y   I N   T H E   U K

JANUARY 27: 'It' #122 runs another article on the committal proceedings and forthcoming trial;

STOKE NEWINGTON: TWO'S COMPANY, THREE'S A CONSPIRACY

It used to be said you were innocent until proven guilty. Recently there seems to have been a subtle change in this principle. Now the idea gaining in popularity is that if the pigs arrest you you're guilty, even though juries may sometimes be stupid enough to find you innocent. Nowhere is this new thinking better illustrated than in the 'Angry Brigade' prosecutions. So certain were Commander Bond and his gang of Ian & Jake's guilt that they were kept in prison for 9 months while still technically innocent. The fact that Ian was eventually found not guilty of bombing charges by a jury has not deterred the police from continuing to oppose bail in the cases of 8 more 'conspirators', 6 of whom have been held since last August.

It's true that charges have been dropped against Chris Allen and Pauline Conroy who were arrested in November. But the carefully emphasised phrase 'at this stage' makes it clear that the pigs still believe them guilty and are waiting for more evidence rather than risking them being found innocent. And although Kate McLean arrested 18 December, was eventually let out on £20,000 bail (not an easy sum to find), this was despite police objections, and on condition of virtual house arrest. The other 3 women are still inside, on the grounds that their release would enable them to 'perpetuate the conspiracy'. Once again, they have yet to be found guilty of conspiring. Naturally the pigs believe the defendants to be guilty, but they still have to prove this to a jury. And they shouldn't be able to penalise defendants chances of proving their innocence. But this is what is happening. And with the help of the courts, who are supposedly neutral.

Why, for instance, were the names of Jim Greenfield, Anna Mendelson, John Barker, Hilary Creek (arrested at Amhurst Rd on 20 August) and Stuart Christie and Chris Bott (arrested visiting the house the next day) allowed to be included in the Prescott-Purdie conspiracy charges on the day of the trial, with the result that the prosecution could 'prove' their guilt, and then by implication, Jake and Ian's. Also, in the P.P. trial, why was the prosecution counsel allowed to quote 27 'outrages', despite Jake only being charged with 2 specific bombings and to draw no meaningful connection between most of them? And why was he allowed to say 'the Stoke Newington 6 were clearly guilty' and 'if you find the evidence is overwhelming that those persons arrested in August were some of the persons responsible anyway for those bombings' (Jake and Ian must also be guilty). Yet they were and still are legally innocent, they were not allowed to answer the charges made in the P.P. trial, and statements made in it are not admissible in their own trial.

This was clearly prejudicial to the current committal proceedings and ultimately to a jury trial. But equally prejudicial in a different way is the denial of bail. A letter from Brixton explains, 'It splits us up. Naturally under their system, it first means women and men are divided, which is simply destructive, unnatural, we are cut off from our bodies, which become things, to perform certain routines and nothing else. And because this all-male world is unnatural, it's unreal as well. To that extent, I am no longer myself, just a part.'

He goes on, 'In terms of preparing a coherent joint defence (conspiracy is a joint charge) everything is made many times more difficult. We have had a few joint meetings, closely observed through glass - yes, because in this world touch is subversive because it makes prisoners into whole people. We have just heard that now we are to have no more joint meetings, at all. These decisions are at a level no doubt made by some little man in the Home Office who has never done one creative thing in the whole of his life.

'We have been physically isolated to try and make our defence into isolated defence cases, as the State would like it. It would, for one thing, be doing it their way. Divide and rule, working on many different levels. This is the way QCs work, defending their client alone, never mind how much such a course means throwing dirt on the other innocent defendants. Also QCs are autocratic, resenting and preventing any control of them by their clients.

'What I am saying is this - the Mangrove 9 and the Chicago 7 did great things in not bowing down to the tyranny of the legal system. The prison remand weapon of the State is being used to try and prevent any such solid joint defence. And this is true not just for us, but for many people in here... The lousy truth is, that since we are powerless in here, we do to a degree become dependant on other 'experts' called solicitors, not because of their knowledge or efficiency, but to arrange any joint meetings. We have no relation of our own to the outside world except for 15 minutes through plate glass.'

However, should any of the defendants choose at any stage to defend himself he would be permanently denied legal aid. Thus the legal profession protects itself. And the Stoke Newington people have to rely on lawyers who turn up once a week or else send junior clerks, and who at joint meetings are in the habit of ignoring the women's ideas in favour of the men's. And living conditions in prison could hardly be described as conducive to concentrated work. Lighting in Holloway consists of one naked lightbulb, controlled by the screws. Anna, who's been inside since August, now finds she can only read about 50 pages of a book before her eyes give out.

While committal proceedings continue, the women miss the last meal of the day and would only be given one sandwich a day if friends didn't send in a meal at lunch-time. They also have to take all their personal possessions with them to court, because screws have turned over their cells in their absence. This is the way in which the prison authorities work with the police to prevent a defendant preparing a satisfactory defence. If this wasn't enough, the co-operation of the Home

Office in banning joint meetings of defendants in prison and of the courts in accepting police requests for bail to be denied and in rushing back to prison at the end of the day, despite promises that defendants would be allowed joint conferences before leaving.

Everything about the court works against them just as much as the police, the prisons or the Home Office. The cells they're locked in at lunchtime are so dark that reading or writing is impossible, and the only food they're given is a sandwich and a cup of tea. Anna, Kate and Hilary have all charged the pigs with assaulting them on the way from the court to the van, but the authorities have found it impossible to identify the pigs in question.

The absolute power of the court is seldom challenged by the defence lawyers. When it is, magistrate Beaumont seldom takes any notice except to get annoyed. Lord Gifford, speaking for Pauline on her release, made a number of requests. He asked that property stolen from her flat by the police be returned. Beaumont refused when prosecutor Dorian Williams pointed out that charges were only being dropped 'at this stage'. Gifford asked that Pauline's telephone not be tapped. Beaumont said he had no power in this direction. He asked that all her prints be destroyed. Beaumont said this was normal police procedure, such was his confidence in them.

Finally Gifford asked that in view of the constant harassment Pauline had received at the hands of the police, pigs Bond and Mould should be bound over to keep the peace. Beaumont was shocked at the suggestion - 'The application is one that I have never heard equalled in 25 years in courts up and down the country for effrontery.' Beaumont did however grant Pauline £150 to pay her lawyers with. After all, why should they be penalised, they've done nothing wrong!

Technically, the idea of committal proceedings is that the pigs are expected to show the magistrate they have a case worth taking before a judge and jury. It's hard to believe that Beaumont will take much convincing, especially since it was he who made 20 Endell Street squatters spend weeks in jail because he insisted that sureties for bail must attend court in London. It was also he who gave George Joseph of the Black Unity and Freedom Party 9 months suspended for 3 years for, as the defence put it, restraining a policeman from using his baton on a black girl.

All of this is only to touch on the main obstructions in the way of the Stoke Newington people, and only illustrates the whole attitude of the authorities, especially the police, towards 'law' and 'justice'. No doubt when the trial of the Stoke Newington 8 does come, the pigs will try to prejudice the result even further, as they did in Jake and Ian's trial with spectacular raids which produced no results, and arrests of people who are later released. The only slim hope is that a jury will be able to wade through the bullshit and see that the use of vague conspiracy charges is only a trick to veil the lack of evidence that the 8 were all responsible for actual bombings.

'There are still eight of us there,' says one of the women, 'there on charges of a very thinly disguised political nature. They rest in most cases on the flimsiest of evidence, and the central thread of their attack - the conspiracy being the basis upon which all repressive regimes, operating in a paranoid manner, react. React to smash their political opposition in a criminal court. It's up to us, the movement and the people as represented through the jury, to have this kicked out.' And you might add, to show who the real conspirators are.

JANUARY 30: Bloody Sunday: Paras shoot dead 13 anti-internment demonstrators in Londonderry.

FEBRUARY 1: Bernadette Devlin physically attacks Home Secretary Reggie Maudling, after he claims that snipers fired on troops first. Same day Rhodesia House in London is firebombed.

FEBRUARY 2: The British Embassy in Dublin is set ablaze and crowds stop fire engines reaching it in time to save it.

FEBRUARY 3: 'Daily Express' headline reads; 'ANARCHY! BRITAIN FEARS COLLAPSE OF DUBLIN GOVERNMENT AND IRA MOB RULE'. Same day Army Recruiting Office in Kirkgate, Huddersfield destroyed in firebomb attack. Also around this time Carlos the Jackal moves in at Phillimore Court on Kensington High Street, just down the road from Biba's. And even Paul McCartney's Wings' new single is entitled 'Give Ireland Back to the Irish'. Cor blimey.

FEBRUARY 4: The weekly underground paper 'Ink' reports on the forthcoming trial;

STOKE NEWINGTON 8: DEFENDANTS LASH OUT

All of the Stoke Newington 8 have been committed for trial at the Old Bailey, despite strong defence submissions that 2 of the defendants, Angela Weir and Kate McLean, had no case to answer. All 8 are charged with conspiring to cause explosions; there are various lesser charges. A late charge of 'conspiracy to steal' brought against some of the defendants on absurd evidence - letters and notes referring to the need to get money - was thrown out by magistrate Beaumont.

Five of the eight made speeches from the dock at the end of the proceedings, after press restrictions were lifted at their own request. However, the pig press didn't manage to report these speeches (although the Daily Telegraph illegally printed details of the prosecution evidence). They pointed out that they had already been tried in their absence during the Prescott-Purdie trial and that Prescott had been convicted largely on the basis of his association with them, although they were not present to defend themselves. They protested that they were being systematically obstructed in the preparation of their defence by the refusal of the prison authorities to let them share cells or have joint conferences, the inspection of all the notes they make, the withholding of documents seized from their flat which are not consistent with the conspiracy charge and in fact contradict it, and the refusal of bail. They pointed out that the various arms of state violence - police, courts, prisons and Home Office - were lying when they pretended that they acted independently. In fact they were conspiring together to get a conviction by any means. They accused the magistrate of acquiescing to this conspiracy.

The fate of the eight should be followed closely. It reveals some of the methods which will be used increasingly against militants and some of the police personnel who will be using them. One of these methods is remands in custody, in itself a punishment before a trial. And the seemingly petty constraints and restrictions of the prison regime form a system whose function is to prevent 'innocent until proven guilty' prisoners from being able to properly defend themselves. Another method is the evidence of police 'experts' whose techniques and qualifications (if any) are incomprehensible to juries. (It would seem a bit far-fetched to suppose that 20 years experience as a police expert gives a man some claim to be impartial.) Another technique is the infamous conspiracy charge itself, which allows the police to build a 'case' out of evidence about your friends and political views. (Industrial militants should watch out for this one.)

The transformation of bail into exile and even house arrest also needs watching. When people are arrested on 'conspiracy' evidence so weak that magistrates feel they have to give bail despite the frightened grunts of the police, highly restrictive bail conditions can be imposed: reporting twice daily to a particular police station, no political activity, spending every night at a particular address. Three defendants in the present case (Angela Weir, Hilary Creek, Kate McLean) are bailed on condition that they live at their parents' homes and do not come within a 20-mile radius of Charing Cross. The original police demand was that they should be restricted to a 15-mile radius around their houses. The legal basis for this is the 1967 Criminal Justice Act, which allows courts to impose bail conditions which appear to be necessary 'in the interests of justice or for the prevention of crime'. It has been pointed out that this opens the way to a system of house arrest and exile like that used in fascist countries. Of course, indefinite detention without trial already exists in one part of the UK. WATCH OUT... It's all part of the drift: Heath's 'quiet revolution'. As more people effectively challenge the system, the ruling class sharpens its teeth. A drift towards the fascism our parents fought a war against. Keep an eye on pigs like Habershon, Bond, Mould, Creamer and their as yet unidentified co-conspirators in Special Branch, intelligence and the Home Office. When they've finished with this spot of bother, they might get interested in YOU. (PS. 'Ink' is described in 'Underground' by Alison Fell of 'Oz' as being; 'very Angry Brigade-ish, anti-imperialist, it had black voices, women's voices, it really did represent that new libertarian/situationist nexus of politics.')

FEBRUARY 17: A bomb blast causes extensive damage to Edge Lane Army HQ in Liverpool. While back in London the Bonhill Street Social Security Office is firebombed. 'Telegram Sam' by T. Rex is at No. 1.

FEBRUARY 22: 7 squaddies killed in IRA Bloody Sunday revenge bombing of Paras HQ at Aldershot.

MARCH 2: German police shoot dead suspected terrorist Tommy Weisbecker. Michael X captured in Guyana and flown back to Trinidad on murder charge.

MARCH 10: Another firebomb attack on South African Airways London office.

MARCH 15: A prison officer is shot outside Wandsworth Prison.

MARCH 20: Shots fired at Army Recruiting Office in Slough.

MARCH 30: A bomb consisting of 13 sticks of gelignite is left on a railway track near Stranraer, frequently used by Army to transport men and munitions to Northern Ireland. Same day heavy sentences dished out to politically motivated Scottish bank robbers.

APRIL: Another bomb found at rail link near Glasgow and a 15 year old boy is arrested for planting a bomb at a police station in Sleaford, Lancs.

MAY: Meanwhile, in the States, a Weathermen bomb explodes in a bathroom in the Pentagon. Fucking A. And in West Germany 4 American GIs are killed and many more injured in RAF anti-Vietnam war bombing campaign. Back in blighty, there's a state of emergency with flying picket miners strike action and Piccadilly virtually blacked out.

THE PROSECUTION

OPENING STATEMENTS - ASSOCIATED SETS AND CONSPIRACIES - GUN GIRL SLEEPS BESIDE ARSENAL - YOU ARE THE FRONT PAGE

MAY 30: As Andreas Baader is captured in Frankfurt and the Japanese Red Army/PFLP massacre 26 at Lod airport, 'Metal Guru' by T. Rex gets to No. 1 and the Trial of the Stoke Newington 8 begins in Number 1 Court of the Central Criminal Court at the Old Bailey. Mendelson and Barker immediately apply to the judge, Justice James, to have the trial postponed for 2 years, because the sensational press coverage is bound to influence the jury. As a compromise, Justice James grants the defence the right to vet the jury. A list of questions is subsequently drawn up to weed out Conservatives, relatives of servicemen in Northern Ireland, and people associated with Angry Brigade target groups. As a result, 17 would-be

jurors drop out because they say they would be biased, 37 are challenged by the defence and 2 by the Crown; leaving a 'broadly working-class' jury, including 5 unemployed. Barker, Creek and Mendelson elect to conduct their own defence, with the assistance of 'McKenzie' helpers (in the form of mates from the underground scene). Greenfield is represented by Ian McDonald, Christie by Kevin Winstain and Patrick Mullen, Kate McLean by Ted Glasgow and Joe Harper, and Angela Weir by Mike Mansfield.

Cue the music: Prosecution counsel, John Mathew opens proceedings by introducing the defendants to the jury and describing the case against them thus;

"The allegation in this case is that these 8 defendants, calling themselves revolutionaries and anarchists, under various names, sought to disrupt and attack the democratic society of this country with whose structure and politics they apparently disagree. To disrupt it by a wave of violent attacks over quite a lengthy period; that is, by causing explosions aimed at the property of those whom they considered to be their political or social opponents..."

Mathew then outlines the various attacks, from 1st of May Group to Angry Brigade, before attempting to explain the conspiracy charge. Then he runs through the individual charges against Greenfield, Mendelson and Christie, which are a bit more straightforward. The conspiracy charge, the main meat of the trial, is to be presented in 3 stages; firstly the 25 attacks have to be linked together; then connected with the evidence found at Amhurst Road; and then with the 8 themselves. But, in effect, the prosecution has only to prove that the defendants have something to do with one of the attacks to make the charge stick.

Mathew's opening statement takes 2 days. Then there's another 107 days to go. The trial is to be the longest and most complicated in the history of the Old Bailey. Even surpassing the previous year's 'Oz' trial. There are 688 exhibits and over 200 prosecution witnesses lined up. The first major witnesses to take the stand are Howard Yallop and Donald Lidstone, from the Woolwich Arsenal explosives lab. They begin by explaining how they linked the various bombs together and singled them out from the thousand plus cases they dealt with between 1967 and 1971. In all 109 are classified as 'infernal machines', intended to damage property.

According to Yallop and Lidstone the 25 AB bombs fall roughly into 2 categories. 17 operate on an acid-delay system, where Sulphuric acid drips onto sugar and potassium chlorate, igniting a detonator set in the explosive. Then there's 6 time-bombs, which operate by a clock hand touching a wire, leading to a battery, which puts a current through the detonator, setting off the explosive. To illustrate their case, the forensics boys present a complex chart of the corresponding elements of the 25 bombs (such as alarm clocks and Ever Ready batteries).

The defence calls Dr. Roy Cahill, an expert on associated sets, to refute the reliability of the chart, because it relies too much on inference. Cahill agrees with Yallop that the 25 bombs are different to all the others but disagrees that they come from the same source. Then Greenfield's counsel, Ian McDonald brings in the 75 year old chemistry and explosives expert, Colonel Shaw to dismiss the whole analysis procedure used at Woolwich. Mainly because no back-up tests had been made or control swabs taken around the explosions.

After a couple of days of forensic evidence and cross-examination, Commander

Bond takes the stand and the defence first puts forward its counter-conspiracy case: that the Amhurst Road bust was a political frame-up to make an example of the 8 to anyone questioning authority. Bond and Habershon naturally insist that their investigation techniques are within the bounds of normal police procedure. Bond goes on to admit that he regards the Angry Brigade as 'an idea that anyone can join', rather than an organisation. Anna Mendelson then pulls him up on his definition of 'anarchists and self-styled revolutionaries'.

Worse is to come for Bond when he's cross-examined about the interrogation of the 8 at Albany Street. John Barker disputes just about everything the police claim he said. But Bond flatly denies that Barker said anything about being framed at the time. Habershon is given an even rougher ride than Bond. Then Sergeants Gilham and Davies are grilled about the actual raid. Gilham is on the witness stand for a whole week. Barker claims that he and Hilary Creek were taken downstairs twice, the first time after Greenfield and Mendelson were taken away, then he claims they were brought back up to the flat and shown the guns and explosives.

The crucial cross-examination of the arresting officers goes on for a month and includes Stuart Christie's lawyer, Kevin Winstain, accusing Gilham of pocketing 2 of the detonators and planting them in Christie's car at Stoke Newington police station. Next up the validity of the conspiracy charge is brought into question. Ted Glasgow, representing Kate McLean, quotes the prosecution as saying; "the sort of conspiracy we have here is of a continuing series of events, which, if proved, is a conspiracy people can come in and out of." Mike Mansfield, representing Angela Weir, adds that the prosecution have merely presented an associated set, which isn't the same thing as a conspiracy. As well as the defence team Mathew has to contend with Habershon hassling him with notes throughout the trial.

In defence of the conspiracy charge, Mathew argues that the count will still be good if the jury comes to the conclusion that only two of the defendants were involved in the conspiracy. According to Mathew the only way the count could be found bad is if there's a central figure in the conspiracy and all the defendants are unknown to each other. Greenfield's counsel, Ian McDonald counters that, "The Crown can't have it's cake and eat it." Either the original 1968-71 conspiracy charge has to be proven (and the defendants found to be participants in it) or the count is bad. But the judge rejects the defence submissions and saves his pronouncement on the rival conspiracy theories until his summing up.

Elsewhere, the Army clears barricades from No Go areas in Londonderry in 'Operation Motorman', German police shoot dead ex. pat. Scot Ian MacLeod by mistake during RAF round-up, the first Ugandan Asians arrive in Britain and 5 striking dockers, the 'Pentonville 5', become the first people to be jailed under the Industrial Relations bill. While in the charts, '20 Dynamite Hits' by Various Artists (no kidding) replaces 'Exile on Main Street' as No. 1 album.

JULY: After headlines such as 'Gun Girl Sleeps Beside Arsenal', during Mathew's opening statement, the trial drops out of the news and there's talk of another press blackout. The presentation of a birthday cake to Anna Mendelson receives a bit of good publicity and light relief, then the anarchist poet/scientist Alex Comfort (of 'Joy of Sex' fame) illicits some radio and TV coverage when he writes to 'The Guardian' regarding the lack of publicity. Albert Meltzer subsequently reports on press coverage of the trial so far, in 'Black Flag' Vol 2 #13;

HOW IS THE TRIAL GOING?

The trial of the 'Stoke Newington 8' sometimes called the 'Angry Brigade Trial' opened - after the defendants had been in custody since August - a week early. It has been going on for over a month at the time of writing. It will continue through the summer (with a break of 3 weeks holiday for all but the defendants) and if it finishes this year we shall be lucky.

Why is it taking so long? It is not an abstract case involving company law, nor are there complicated questions to argue. The prosecution are taking so long to argue their case because it has weight (avoirdupois) but not substance. It is not for us to comment while the case is sub judice though everyone else is doing so. But we will take a look at the Press.

The case opened to a rush of headlines. The 'quality' papers reported the allegations made by the prosecution in full. The 'Telegraph' reported these, and subsequent allegations, repeating the phrase that the accused wanted to 'disrupt society' several times. But as the prosecution witnesses appeared and either gave evidence favourable to the accused, or were dismissed as fools or liars, no word appeared. The 'Guardian' and to a lesser extent the 'Times' did report some of these changes. The fact that a copy of the 'Standard' (a vital piece of police evidence) had been destroyed because the police did not have room to store it came over in several papers, including the 'Standard'.

The prosecution's Mr. Mathew's remarks about anarchists who wanted to disrupt society were later described by a witness as 'Tory prejudice'. This wasn't reported. The average newspaper might be forgiven for thinking it was a strange verdict if at the finish the accused were acquitted. At the moment many think the case is over. While Special Branch make such a bad showing in the box, nothing is reported. Mr. Palmer-Hall refused to answer questions on Special Branch activity and was asked by John Barker if the reason he refused was because he was undertaking illegal Special Branch activities. "I can't comment on that" he replied. Best reports come in 'Time Out'. It is criticised by many of our friends as commercial. So it is. Precisely because it wants to sell, it doesn't flout its readers' opinions audaciously. Its coverage is reasonable and it's only a pity it's confined to London.

Lawyers. There has been a lot in the Press about the absence of QCs. 'Free Society' published a prejudicial report, in which among other things it suggested that QCs had refused to take the case because they disliked the politics of the accused. Nobody has alleged that. Many QCs refused to act because they were frightened of the political police, which is another matter. (One professional man candidly admitted he would not give vital forensic evidence because, he said in private, he was afraid of what would happen.) It is a pity there should be any criticism of those who are representing the accused. They may explode the myth that QCs are essential. THE CASE CONTINUES.

AUGUST: After Justice James gives everybody a month's holiday, there's another sit-in prison reform demo in Brixton's 'A' Wing, involving Barker, Bott, Christie and Greenfield. In Port of Spain Michael X is sentenced to death for murder. Summer of '72 hits include; 'Children of the Revolution' by T. Rex, 'School's Out' by Alice Cooper, 'All the Young Dudes' by Mott the Hoople, 'Silver Machine' by Lemmy's Hawkwind, 'Mama Weer All Crazee Now' by Slade, and the Munich Olympic village by Black September.

SEPTEMBER: The Stoke Newington 8 Defence Bulletin reads;

THE TRIAL SO FAR... Has been 4 months of prosecution, 4 months of police witness after witness contradicting each other, changing their story, LYING, broken only for four weeks when the judge had his holiday... A CONSPIRACY OF SILENCE. The Press have reported nothing of all this - just as they never reported the bombings until it suited them. What are they scared of? WHAT CONSPIRACY? The only concrete evidence is the guns and gelignite 'found' by the police in the flat where 4 of the defendants lived. At first the police said that 2 of the 4 were there throughout the raid; then they admitted that at one point they were taken out of the flat then brought back. WHY? The fingerprint expert admitted that there were no prints on the guns and explosives. WHY NOT? The prosecution's story changed from day to day. It emerged that the police would have fallen flat over the guns and gelly as they came into the flat if it had been where they said it was, instead of 'finding' it ten minutes later; so they suddenly 'remembered' for the first time - a year later - that it had been covered with clothes. POLICE CONSPIRACY. One detective was forced to admit that he had altered his notebook during the trial. Another gave the game away altogether when he said that he and a colleague sat down in the kitchen and 'decided' what happened in the raid. NO CONSPIRACY. The rest of the evidence against the eight is research, letters and articles written by the defendants for different underground papers ('Frendz', 'Strike') and broadsheets. The prosecution call them proof of conspiracy because they mention such political targets as the Industrial Relations Act, Fair Rents Act, Miss World contest, etc. Their scientific experts tried to pin 25 of the bombings that took place in England between 1968 and 1971 onto these people, claiming that these bombings were 'associated' - disregarding other similar bombings and covering up the differences between the 25. But the explosions were claimed by groups as different as the 1st of May group, the Angry Brigade, the Wild Bunch and Butch Cassidy and the Sundance Kid. And the 'set' didn't include 3 claimed by the Angry Brigade AFTER Amhurst Road was raided. Now the defence is beginning, the truth can come out: the only conspiracy there's been is a STATE CONSPIRACY.

The Stoke Newington 8 Defence Group is run out of Compendium bookshop at 240 Camden High Street. Which leads to a thinly disguised Angry Brigade episode of ITV's 'Special Branch', with a foreign agent working undercover in a radical bookshop. As the script puts it; 'He's got a Swiss bank account, he's the owner of Compendium bookshop, he's a known homosexual.' Compendium owner Nicholas Rochford subsequently sues and receives £7,000 damages. John Barker says the Stoke Newington 8 Defence Group is more interesting/exciting than the actual Angry Brigade.

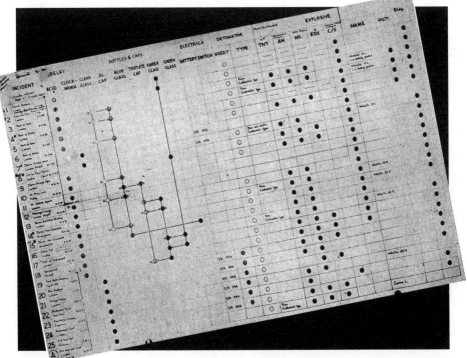

Woolwich Forensic Lab chart linking the 25 bombs together.

Illustration by Roy Knipe. Research by a cast of thousands.

The Stoke Newington 8

All of the 'Stoke Newington 8' deny the charges against them. All the defendants who have given evidence have attacked terrorism — and have seen the Angry Brigade as fairly irrelevant to the class struggle. But they have recognized the Angry Brigade's actions as reflecting the feelings of thousands. They have described their involvement in squatting and Claimants Union activities, and now this presents them to the police as plausible culprits. The proceedings are smothered with a tight security blanket around the court and a virtual blackout by the national press. Those whom the state wishes to destroy, it first renders anonymous...

The defendants:
Top, left to right: John Barker, Chris Bott, Angela Weir, Stuart Christie.
Bottom, left to right: Kate McLean, Anna Mendleson, Hilary Creek, Jim Greenfield.

'Oz' #45, November 1972.

THE DEFENCE

CHILDREN OF THE REVOLUTION - THE POWERS THAT BE - BOMB CULTURE - WHEN YOU TALK ABOUT DESTRUCTION YOU CAN COUNT ME OUT...IN

OCTOBER 3: After 3 months of prosecution evidence, Ian McDonald kicks off the defence, on behalf of not only Greenfield but unofficially the others as well. He stresses how unusual the case is and how important political motive is to it. Because the prosecution has little or no evidence about the actual perpetrators of the 25 bombings. And has to prove that the defendants are capable of the bombings and not just the most likely suspects to make an example of;

"If the powers that be have their way, then your task is to convict these defendants - maybe letting off one or two of the peripheral ones - and then the press and everyone can bray triumphantly about how successful the police have been in tracking down these red hippie hooligans, or whatever other epithets Fleet Street think up in describing them. Make no mistake, that is what the powers that be expected and hope for in this case. Your co-operation is part of that overall strategy. And I believe that is what is expected of you in this case. You probably realise by now that the verdict you have to give in this trial is of concern to more people than simply the relatives of those in the dock. You probably realise that the whole British Establishment awaits your verdict with bated breath. You and the defendants, when you really consider it, are the only unpredictable factors in this whole scenario. The rest of us can be expected to play our allotted parts. That gives you enormous power. It is your decision, and your decision alone, that decides the outcome of this case."

Following McDonald's opening statement, Jim Greenfield is called to the witness box, to go through his life story, what he was doing at the time of the bombings and where he stands politically. Greenfield talks about his involvement with

'Strike' and admits to having sympathy for the Angry Brigade, but says he disapproves of the bombings because they haven't helped the working class struggle. As for the Angry Brigade stuff found at Amhurst Road, each of the defendants gives the same explanation: They admit that two people with Angry Brigade connections used the duplicator at the flat to copy Communique 11. They sent Greenfield an incriminating document on guns and explosives. Then the police came to know about Amhurst Road, acquired the arms cache and duly planted it. All the information seized on big companies and lists of prominent people is merely 'reverse-sociology' material for a series of pamphlets. Mathew's subsequent cross-examination of 'the technical expert' Greenfield homes in on the two people with Angry Brigade connections;

Mathew: "Well, Mr. Greenfield, who are these two mysterious people who suddenly turn up at 359 Amhurst Road?"
Greenfield: "I don't intend to tell you."
Mathew: "Why is that?"
Greenfield: "Because I don't feel they should be put in the position I am in now."
Mathew: "But it is they who have largely contributed, if there is a word of truth in what you say, they are the people who have largely contributed to you being where you are today."
Greenfield: "The people who are responsible for putting me where I am today are the policemen who planted all the..."
Mathew: "All the incriminating property found at Amhurst Road... Why do you wish to protect them, Mr. Greenfield?"
Greenfield: "I wish to protect them because, criticism aside of the Angry Brigade, what they may have done, what they may have had in mind, criticism of that aside, in opposition to you, they are on my side."
Mathew: "Terrorists?"
Greenfield: "No, I wouldn't say they are terrorists, but it is open to debate."
Mathew: "You, Mr. Greenfield, using violence by bombing, if you thought that would have helped your ideals, would you have resorted to it?"
Greenfield: "I wasn't interested in advancing my ideals."
Mathew: "I thought you had been telling us very little else for the past two days. You left university and did very little work just to do this."
Greenfield: "What I have done is attempting over the last few years to live and act in a way that I would call socialist. I am not interested in propagating my ideals."
Mathew: "Would I be right in suggesting that you didn't want to tell us the names of the two people, and what you have said is quite untrue?"
Greenfield: "You are getting paid to say that. What I have said is perfectly true."
Mathew: "The reason you won't tell us these names is because you know that what you have said in this court is quite untrue."

Greenfield: "I know that I have told the truth."

Mathew: "One other general matter before we come down to the facts in this case. I don't think we have argued about this. You have a hatred of the police, haven't you?"

Greenfield: "No, what I do have is, I have had certain experiences which allow me to put the police in perspective inside the modern state, and I see how and why they do certain things."

Mathew: "And are you telling this court that as far as you are concerned you don't hate the police?"

Greenfield: "I hate the people who came to Amhurst Road and planted us with guns and explosives. In general, I don't hate the police at all."

Mathew: "You had some unfortunate experiences at Widnes when you were arrested..."

Greenfield: "Yes."

Mathew: "And in August?"

Greenfield: "Yes."

Mathew: "And you saw some unhappy things happening at Notting Hill Gate."

Greenfield: "Unhappy!"

Mathew: "Did you see unhappy things happen?"

Greenfield: "I would say it was downright disgusting."

Mathew: "That is what I thought you would say. You hate the police."

Greenfield: "That is not enough."

Mathew: "And when you started to put together this periodical called 'Strike' you were dealing with matters under the heading 'Repression'."

Greenfield: "Yes."

Mathew: "And what I suggest to you, Mr. Greenfield, is this. That really such is your hatred of the police and authority in general, but particularly the police..."

Greenfield: "What authority?"

Mathew: "I am talking about the police in particular."

Greenfield: "You also mention authority, and I would like to know which authority you mean?"

Mathew: "Unfortunately you will interrupt when I haven't finished the question. You see, Mr. Greenfield, you really have to dispute and attack the police in everything they say and do as you have in this case."

Greenfield: "I have to do it because everything they say and do that I have disputed is fabricated."

Next in the witness box is 'the Ideologist' John Barker, who remains unassisted by counsel throughout his cross-examination. Barker begins his defence by reading a 10,000 word statement, describing his political influences, his involvement with the Claimants Union and what he thinks of the Angry Brigade;

"I thought what was wrong with the Angry Brigade was that it didn't seem to be a general campaign or strategy, and I have always believed that the only way you are going to get anywhere worthwhile is when a lot of people have actually reached the stage in their everyday experience of wanting to use class violence. They can't just say we are going to introduce it and see what happens because that is what I call elitism, they are saying that we have decided to do this and see what will happen completely out of time with what is happening generally. Mainly I think despite all my political criticisms, I did respect the people in the Angry Brigade because they were at least putting into practice what they thought to be right or what they believed to be happening at that time, but I came to the conclusion that really I couldn't become a part of it (i) because I didn't really have the necessary kind of experience, and (ii) because I thought it would be a full time thing, and I certainly don't believe that what the Angry Brigade is doing is worth doing full time, and thirdly I ask myself the question, is this the time to do this sort of thing, and I came to the conclusion that it wasn't and that all that it was really producing was an excuse for a terrible amount of repression amongst people who had the same kind of ideas on the same kind of thing as myself."

Barker goes on to admit that he had considered robbery but hadn't taken it any further than that. His explanation for the Boulogne trip is that he merely acted as a messenger for the Angry Brigade people, regarding arrangements for Purdie and Prescott if they were sprung from prison. He admits that 'Rosemary Pink' is not the real name of the girl who accompanied him on the trip, but flatly denies it was Angela Weir. Christie 'The Ringleader / Mr. Big' gets grilled about his 1st of May connections, which stem from a slightly incriminating letter plus a screwdriver with traces of explosive, and why he thought he could borrow money off Barker who was reduced to busking at the time. Angela Weir produces evidence that she was attending a Gay Liberation march at the time of the Boulogne trip (refuting the prosecution evidence: a picture resembling her on a 24 hour BR excursion card which corresponds with a ticket found at Amhurst Road). Kate McLean, who only has similar handwriting (to the 'Dear Boss' communique) against her, and Chris Bott don't go into the witness box at all.

OCTOBER 29: The 3 surviving Munich massacre terrorists are released after Black September Lufthansa hijacking between Beirut and Ankara. Throughout 1972 there are a total of 61 attempted plane hijackings.

NOVEMBER: The defendants are finally allowed to have meetings at Brixton to prepare their closing speeches. Anna Mendelson (cast as 'Greenfield's Moll' by the prosecution) makes hers first. She has been ill throughout the trial, as has Hilary Creek, and has to take several breaks. Basically she says the police set them up because of their alternative lifestyle and political stance. She doesn't deny having connections with the Angry Brigade, or to writing part of the Moonlighters'

Cell Communique (in opposition to internment in Northern Ireland), because that's the political circles she moves in. As for the copy of 'Rolling Stone' with her fingerprints on it, which was in the bag containing the Manchester bomb;

"The doors were open, people were always coming in, and half the time you didn't know who they were. There were a lot of strangers around... and fingerprints can get on a piece of paper in a million different ways. I can't account for that, and I can't say how it got there. I suppose it just comes down to whether you believe me. I wasn't making bombs...

"Our sort of people, our politics, the people living in Amhurst Road, we didn't and we don't feel that there is any need or room for bomb attacks on cabinet ministers, although we might understand the feelings behind them. Bombing a cabinet minister isn't going to get rid of the capitalist system, because there is always somebody to step into his place unless the situation and conditions are right."

Then it's John Barker with the definitive speech of the trial, which causes one lawyer to comment that top briefs get paid £20,000 a year for doing what Barker is doing for the first time. He delivers a convincing case for the police frame up theory and casts at least some doubt on the authorities' motives;

"The appearance of arresting people is as important, if not more important, than actually smashing the Angry Brigade itself. It's the whole question of setting an example. Showing people that they can't get away with it. But of course, if that is the case, they may still be worried about the real Angry Brigade, perhaps they are still looking for it. They still have a large Bomb Squad which doesn't seem to have changed much in size from when we were arrested... Perhaps they (the Angry Brigade) now feel that bombs are completely irrelevant, and that the class war is being fought, and that the Angry Brigade doesn't have to make symbolic gestures with bombs to make it real, because it is real."

After Barker, Hilary Creek, who's been cast as 'the Go-between', expands on the plant conspiracy and accuses the prosecution of turning their legitimate political activities into evidence, effectively putting them on trial for their idea(l)s. She finishes by saying;

"Although they might have been getting close with us, the fact still remains that they got the wrong people, and that's not good enough."

The closing statements of the Amhurst 4 take 8 days to deliver. Then counsel for the other 4, Christie, Bott, Weir and McLean quickly reiterate their respective defence cases and that's it. There's just the judge's summing up to go.

WHOSE CONSPIRACY?

THE END OF THE AFFAIR? - THE SUMMING UP - THIS IS NOT A POLITICAL TRIAL - ANGRY ABOUT BEING ON TRIAL - MAMA WEER ALL CRAZEE NOW

NOVEMBER 24: Justice James, begins his summing up. First he establishes that his interpretation of the law is absolute. But the jury can agree or disagree with his suggestions 'to help them as to the facts'. Then he admits that 'lifestyle' considerations are an issue in the trial and directs the jury to base their judgments on "truth, accuracy and credibility. Because some people are lying in this case, and there's no getting away from that." He reminds the jury that the burden of proof lays with the prosecution and instructs them to go through the charges in chronological order before dealing with the conspiracy charge.

Basically, it comes down to whether or not the jury believe that the police planted the guns and explosives at Amhurst Road. If they do all the other charges will have to be thrown out. If they don't, the other charges will probably stick as well, including the conspiracy. The prosecution doesn't have to prove that the defendants caused any of the explosions, just that they knew about them;

"As long as you know what the agreement is, then you are a conspirator. You needn't necessarily know your fellow conspirators, nor need you be always active in the conspiracy. All you need to know is the agreement. It can be effected by a wink or a nod, without a word being exchanged. It need have no particular time limit, no particular form, no boundaries."

Justice James then adds that it isn't necessary for the prosecution to prove that the 8 were active in the conspiracy from 1968 to 1971, just at some time during that period. However, he also directs the jury to find the defendants not guilty if they decide there was more than one conspiracy. As for the political angle, he pronounces;

"This is not a political trial. Political trials are trials of people for their political beliefs which happen to be contrary to those in government... We do not have them in this country."

DECEMBER 2: After 8 days Justice James finally completes his summing up, once more outlining the Crown's case;

"In no case does the Crown seek to establish that any of the individuals accused have set off an explosive device or put an explosive device in the place where it was intended to explode. They don't have to establish that anyone did that act in order to convict for the offence of conspiracy. The Crown say that you cannot accept as even reasonably possible the massive dishonesty that would be involved in planting, involving so many police officers from high to low rank, involving such significant coincidences in what was planted at the flat and what was found there otherwise. They say you cannot accept that police perjured themselves to such a degree to cover the wicked assault on Greenfield by three police officers. You cannot accept, they say, the gigantic perjury that would be involved if the allegations made by the defence were right."

EARLY DECEMBER: Robin McGregor reports on the trial in 'It' #142;

ANGRY ABOUT BEING ON TRIAL

January 12th 1971 was a historic day of struggle against the Industrial Relations Bill. 100,000 people marched, and at the Albert Hall there was a mass protest meeting where Harold Wilson was booed and Feather got the bird. About midnight we heard the dramatic news, 'Robert Carr (the author of the Industrial Relations Bill) got it tonight.' Ever since the bombing of Robert Carr's place, and subsequent modification to his kitchen design, carried out by that well known group of demolition experts, the 'Angry Brigade', the hornet's nest of capitalist revenge has been let loose, with a continual spate of police raids looking for 'likely candidates for an outrage,' to use the words of Chief Superintendent Habershon, appointed to 'get results fast' for the establishment. This ritual of revenge, egged on by nervous jumpy cabinet ministers, bosses like Mr. Batty of Fords, and vicious-minded lawmen like Peter Rawlinson, the Attorney-General, whose properties were all Angry Brigade targets, led to the arrest of 6 people at Stoke Newington in August 1971... to be joined in the dock by 2 others, now known as the Stoke Newington Eight trial.

The trial in Court 1 of the Old Bailey has now dragged on since May. The prosecution has thrown in every dirt-scraping scrap of evidence it could muster, leaflets about unemployment, women's liberation, the industrial relations bill, and

mountains of research on property companies in order to support the basic allega-
tion that there has been a single conspiracy to cause 25 explosions, and the charge
of possession of explosives against 4 out of the 8 defendants. Such is the spirit of
revenge against those who sympathise with attacks on ruling class property, that
the actual conspiracy charge reads, 'you did conspire between January 1968 and
August 1971'... Hey brother, can you remember an idle canteen conversation back
in March 1968 about blowing up the bosses? With the prosecution case now finally
finished, the defence has pointed out that in spite of their incredible 1000 pages
plus of evidence, and over 800 exhibits, "the police haven't a clue as to who plant-
ed the bombs in 22 out of the 25 cases."

This is Britain's biggest ever conspiracy trial, and there is a strong defence col-
lective fighting every single one of the thousand plus pages of evidence. Anna
Mendelson, John Barker and Hilary Creek are defending themselves. They have no
lawyers to muffle their arguments, no go-betweens to soften the natural confronta-
tion with class justice. They fight the case with a team of off-beat legal advisors
called 'McKenzies' who have political pride in their lack of bourgeois qualifica-
tions. Their motto is, 'you don't need to be a lawyer to know the law, and to know
the law is bent.' The other 5 are represented by barristers. However, they are
forced to respect the collective solidarity (ie. No deals with the prosecution at any
other defendant's expense).

From the outset the trial has been all about politics. According to British law
there is no such thing as a political trial... there are only 'criminals with political
motives'. This is how his lordship, sitting halfway up the wall of the courtroom
sees it... Judge James declared, "this is not a political trial." However, the defence
insisted on asking the jurors questions about their political prejudices, their rela-
tionship with Securicor, with the police, the armed forces, and the ruling class.
This has never happened before. On this basis the defence scrupulously selected a
100% working class jury, including several unemployed. From their natural class
experience of police repression and establishment violence, the defence puts
across arguments to the jury about government attacks on the working class. The
courtroom struggle inside is sometimes a mirror of the class struggle outside.

The sombre absurdity of the pompous white wigs and black gowns, the ritual
bowing and scraping in front of the judge, the deathly atmosphere of silent reason
and blind justice is daily attacked by John, Anna and Hilary defending themselves,
using the sort of language that ordinary people talk, words that a working class
jury uses. This changes their role in the case from mere passive objects in the
dock, into the active accusers of the prosecution and the state, an eye to eyeball
confrontation with police fabrications. Already John Barker has cited Robert
Mark, the new police chief, for contempt of court, and the Guardian newspaper of
June 22nd reports the Judge's decision on the defendants' application: ie. Mark is
in contempt of court.

The defence has even challenged the establishment experts on explosives and chemistry. The 2 scientists, Yallop and Lidstone, claim that the prosecution's selection of 25 bombings comprises a consistent pattern of chemical make-up. Conveniently all recent political bombing attacks on the government have not been included in their wonderful charts. These experts admitted that several bombings since the arrests fitted their chemical analysis of 'AB' style explosions... but the prosecution did not want to know, because it tends to suggest the police may not have arrested the 'Angry Brigade' at all. When questioned by the defence Lidstone said, "it is part of my job to help the police in any way I can" and "no, I have never given evidence for the defence. I can't have a foot in both camps." The myth of scientific integrity had been attacked and the jury saw them exposed for the government hacks that they are. Now the defence is going to prove that this 'scientific' conspiracy of 25 bombings is completely arbitrary... there are few connections between the machine-gunning of the Spanish Embassy in 1968, and the bombing of Carr's house in 1971. The prosecutor has been overheard grumbling bitterly, "I don't know what's happened to forensic science these days."

Over half the special Angry Brigade bomb squad detectives are Special Branch. Inspector Palmer-Hall, new SB expert on Middle East affairs, admits that he was sent to join the squad by no less than the former head of Special Branch, Deputy Assistant Commissioner Ferguson-Smith. Special Branch in Manchester had kept tabs on the Cannock Street Commune where 4 defendants once lived, and their activity against the Industrial Relations Bill, and their involvement in the Manchester Claimants Union is part of the evidence against them. In the witness-box Special Branch are often amazingly shy about the nature of their work. One after another they say like puppets, "I cannot answer any questions concerning the work of Special Branch", "It is not in the public interest", "I have signed the Official Secrets' Act and therefore cannot divulge confidential information".

One defendant attacked Special Branch Inspector Palmer-Hall, asking, "Is the nature of your work secret because you have special authority to organise illegal operations against political militants? Does Special Branch remain secret because of what happened in the IRA arms trial (reported in the 'Sunday Mirror' and 'Sunday Times' of June 18th) in which Special Branch organised the planting of guns and explosives on the defendants? Instantly the good Inspector blurts out, "I can't answer that question," and then realising too late the mistake, he hastily adds, "NO, CERTAINLY NOT!!" Of course the English secret police would never dream of doing things like that. And so those defending themselves keep putting the awkward questions that lawyers never dare to pose, questions which bring red faces to the courtroom hierarchy, and dithering embarrassment from the witnesses.

Much of the case hangs on the Amhurst Road police raid, a rough crew of detective sergeants and others under their command, claiming that after 50 miserably unsuccessful raids on political militants, suddenly they found the lot.

109

Sergeant Davies and Gilham claimed they found sub-machine guns, gelignite and detonators. The defence has challenged this evidence as total perjury and fabrication. Gilham, Davies and Doyle, from Scotland Yard's central pool of detectives (for top-priority investigations) have been accused of planting the evidence.

The court had been told "the investigation was getting nowhere." Even after the arrest of Purdie and Prescott,.and after Commander X, 'mystery supremo', had been appointed to smash the Angry Brigade on the instructions of the Home Secretary and Waldron, the chief of police, the bombings still continued. In June the Angry Brigade had been declared 'public enemy No. 1' and in August there was still the same catalogue of failure. In the words of Special Branch Sergeant Woolard, "we were getting on very badly." In this way, the defence has tried to prove that the law had the motive for the crime, they had the opportunity, that planting is a well-established police practice, and that the investigation was given the green-light by the cabinet to get results by whatever means necessary. Of course, both sides in the case, the state and the defendants deny all charges. But the defendants are different, they are fighting for their lives... the only things the police officers stand to lose if they don't get convictions is bloody promotion. One officer with more charges to deny than anyone else, whose name crops up all the time, is sitting under the prosecutor's nose, juggling with the evidence. This is Habershon, Chief Superintendent from Barnet, who regards his crusade against the Angry Brigade and their supporters as his biggest case yet. Habershon is like a blustering burly Barlow straight out of Z-Cars... determined to get results and not to let anyone get in the way.

Solicitors get in the way, so 'H' decides no solicitors present during interrogations. People's rights to refuse to go to a police station get in the way, (under section 2 of the 1967 Criminal Justice Act, the police have limited powers to arrest you on 'reasonable grounds of suspicion', but Habershon's tactics of 'arrest for questioning' are definitely illegal), so 'H' decides to grab anyone he feels like detaining for questioning. He tells the court, "I have been keeping law and order for 26 years." For 'H' that includes 25 people wrongfully arrested and falsely imprisoned at Barnet. 'H' accuses defence solicitors of being "all in it together." He views complaints against raids that wreck people's homes and rob them of their address books as "mere ploys to hinder his investigations." Habershon said that on January 12th he had barely heard of the Industrial Relations Bill. But whether the mass of people liked it or not, Habershon and his bully-boys were going to get evidence by gate-crashing people's homes - over 50 raids between January and August. Habershon decides who is guilty, like Robert Mark says, "the police know best."

In a previous trial at which the names of the Stoke Newington 8 were mentioned in their absence in the indictment, Ian Purdie was found not guilty of the same charges. Jack Prescott was acquitted of the bombing charges. The good superin-

tendent then said, "I know a conspiracy when I see one." The defence reckons that through his beady-paranoid eyes he sees conspiracies everywhere... Mr. Bond, chief law and order agent, is well aware of minor threats to the system. 25 bombings... no deaths... one minor injury. Mr. Bond calls this terror, violence and anarchy. But industrial deaths, accidental deaths which result from criminal negligence, Mr. Bond knows nothing about and clearly does not want to know anything. Every day manslaughter by the ruling class is a whole field "outside the scope of my inquiries." A policeman's first job is to protect the state, to hell with the public.

The Defence alleges conspiracy... that the Cabinet plotted in hushed whispers behind locked doors with heads of the secret service to get 'the bombers' or failing that any would-be potential urban guerrillas, or sympathisers. Cast the net wide enough and some group on the Left were bound to be trapped. An incredible struggle is being fought from the cells of Brixton and from house-arrest in Ilford. The pressures and strains are impossible. Yet to be acquitted on all charges is possible. But they need your active support... they can't do it on their own. These comrades need to see your face too in Court 1 of the Public Gallery of the Old Bailey. Be there. Solidarity with the Stoke Newington 8. PS. Send money and get information from the Defence Group, 240 Camden High Street, London NW1. PS. They always tell you that the public gallery is full to keep comrades out. Don't be fooled.

THE VERDICT

ALL THE YOUNG DUDES - DOWNFALL OF THE BIGHEAD BRIGADE - SEX ORGIES AT THE COTTAGE OF BLOOD - DROPOUTS WITH BRAINS TRIED TO LAUNCH A BLOODY REVOLUTION - I FOUGHT THE LAW AND THE LAW WON

DECEMBER 4: After 109 days the hearings end and the jury retires to consider its verdict. By 4.30 the required unanimous verdict isn't forthcoming. So the chief administrator of the Old Bailey arranges to swear in 4 jury bailiffs to look after the jury at a secret nearby hotel. Shortly after 5 the jurors are driven out of the Old Bailey in a minibus with a police escort. Gordon Carr describes the scene in 'The Angry Brigade';

At the end of any major trial, the huge waiting hall outside the various Old Bailey courtrooms takes on something of the atmosphere of a Riviera gambling casino - quiet, tense, with a kind of subdued excitement; at the end of the Angry Brigade hearings, even more so. Special Branch men chatted casually to the reporters covering the trial, speculating on the verdicts, betting on the length of the sentences. In the street outside, a group of 30 or so from the Stoke Newington Eight Defence Group who had done so much work round the trial preparing transcripts, publishing articles, helping to trace witnesses, kept up their vigil, marching with their banners round the public convenience on the traffic island opposite the Judge's entrance.

DECEMBER 5: At midday the jury sends a written question to Justice James asking why the police didn't evacuate Amhurst Road when they found the explosives. The judge replies that the police did stop their search until an explosives expert checked that the explosives were safe. There are no further questions but when the jury returns they tell the judge they're still unable to reach a unanimous verdict.

Bond and Habershon at Scotland Yard press conference after the verdict.

DECEMBER 6: In the end Justice James says he's prepared to accept a majority verdict. The jury retires once more until 5, when they return with their verdict:

John Barker, Jim Greenfield, Anna Mendelson and Hilary Creek are found guilty of conspiring to cause explosions between January 1968 and August 1971, by a majority of 10 to 2: 7 jurors are convinced, 3 are undecided and 2 are not prepared to convict. Greenfield and Mendelson are acquitted on the specific charges of conspiring to cause explosions at Paddington and Manchester. Christie, Bott, Weir and McLean are unanimously acquitted on all counts and discharged. So, in Christie's case at least the jury think the police planted the detonators in his car. Christie ends up with a small fine for driving without a license and the others are released on conviction for the cheque fraud, which they've served more than enough time for already. The jury foreman also makes a point of asking for leniency or clemency. Then Justice James pronounces;

"The conspiracy of which you have been convicted has as its object the intention of disrupting and attacking the democratic society of this country. That was the way it was put by the Crown, and that is the way it has been proved to the satisfac-

113

tion of the jury once the suggestions of planting of evidence had been got rid of on overwhelming evidence.

"The philosophies which you subscribe to are those which are set out in the various Angry Brigade communiques. This conspiracy was alleged to have extended from 1968 until August 1971, but it is clear that the evidence was stronger against you in respect of the latter stages of that period than it was in respect of the earlier stages. For the purposes of sentence, I propose to disregard any of the incidents which occurred before responsibility is claimed by the Angry Brigade communiques. That shortens the period and reduces the number of explosions.

"The means that you adopted could have been even more lethal than they were, but I am satisfied on the evidence that the devices you used were not deliberately designed to cause death or serious injury, but rather damage to property. Nevertheless, in every one of these cases, there was a risk of death or serious injury. Fortunately, only one person suffered any injury. There is, however, evidence that it is fortunate that no one was killed.

"Your participation arose because you objected to the orderly way of society. One of the most precious rights is that an individual should hold his own opinions and be able to express them and be able to protest, and when one finds others who set out to dominate by exercising their opinions to the extent of enforcing them with violence it undermines that precious right.

"I am not going to lecture you. I am sorry to see such educated people in your situation. Undoubtedly a warped understanding of sociology has brought you to the state in which you are. The jury have asked me to take a course which will show mercy. In such a case as this the sentence called for by these offences must be a substantial one, and there are limits to which a court can give effect to such a recommendation, but I will do it to the utmost that I think right.

"I treat you all as persons of good character. You, Greenfield and Barker, have previous convictions, but in dealing with these matters antecedents and previous history can have little effect, save to explain the situations in which you are.

"Undoubtedly you have in many of your interests sought to do good and have done good, and I count that in your favour. But when all is said and done the public is entitled to protection.

"Everyone must know that anyone who seeks to behave in this manner, holding explosives and weapons, must expect severe punishment. I am going to reduce the totality of the sentences, by reason of the jury's recommendation, by 5 years."

Nonetheless, the 4 are still sentenced to 10 years (rather than the mandatory 15) a-piece for conspiracy, to run concurrently with 15 year stretches for possession, As they leave the dock, Mendelson, Barker and Creek thank the 2 jurors "who had faith" in them.

DECEMBER 7: Up to 600 protestors march on Holloway Prison, as the Police name two more people they want in connection with the bombings; Jerry Osner and Sarah Poulikakou from Notting Hill, who are both out of the country. Amongst the post-verdict free for all 'The Sun' comes up with the following;

'Sex Orgies at the Cottage of Blood' comes from a story in the Colchester 'Evening Gazette', where Hilary Creek and Anna Mendelson's former landlord in Wivenhoe, Essex, recalls seeing; 'men and women dressed only in white sheets taking part in strange rituals.' The landlord couldn't confirm; 'reports that revellers had indulged in the sacrificial killing of birds,' (the turkeys Jim Greenfield nicked) but goes onto complain of; 'sacrificial orgies, bizarre sexual activities, anarchist-type meetings, drug taking and unpaid rent bills.' There's also a Hilary Creek topless sunbathing on bail in Wales story, though my favourite is still 'Gun Girl Sleeps beside Arsenal'.

In the 'Daily Telegraph' Maurice Weaver describes the Angry Brigade as a pale imitation of old anarchists like Ravachol and, with the assistance of a psychology professor from Nottingham University, goes onto write;

ANGRY BRIGADE IS CLASSIC CASE FOR SOCIOLOGISTS

Sociologists, psychologists and psychiatrists see the saga of the youngsters with such ordinary domestic pedigrees who suddenly turned to anarchist extremism as one with relevance to the wider picture of student unrest... The divergent but essentially unremarkable backgrounds of the quartet makes the search for any common factor which might have influenced their development a difficult one.

Dr. J.C. Gunn of the Institute of Psychology at London University adds;

The pattern of pressures which have been affecting their actions will obviously be studied and re-studied. One of the factors which must be taken into account is the way they were affected by their exposure to university life. The broader spectrum of society now attending and mixing in universities is creating an entirely new sociological picture.

And a 'senior London Psychiatrist' explains Jim Greenfield *'changing from a very reserved and politically uninterested young boy to a rebel'* thus;

The wider publicity that is given to the wrongs and injustices of the world, together with the effect of mixing with other people from a broad range of society, do have dramatic effect on some undergraduates. The basic arrogance that is demonstrated by these people in their attempts to change the world by violence, often goes side by side with a basic immaturity and an unreadiness to accept affection and worldly realities.

The 'Evening Standard' is slightly hipper than 'The Sun' and 'Telegraph' in reporting;

These guerrillas are the violent activists of a revolution comprising workers, students, teachers, unemployed and women striving for liberation.

Angela Weir complains to 'Time Out' about the traditional Left largely ignoring the trial and the underground making too much of it, and goes on to say; "Now I'm much more convinced of a proper Marxist understanding of the situation, and a strategy which comes from that, and of the need for proper organisation." 'Time Out' comes down on the fence as usual with its cover headline; 'The Verdict of an Uneasy Majority'. While the Manchester/Leeds underground paper 'Mole Express' announces; *'None of us is free while our brothers and sisters are in jail.'* Leaving the 'Daily Express' to have a good gloat and sum up the establishment reaction to the verdict, and the effect the Angry Brigade Anarchy in the UK tour had on it;

THE ANGRY BRIGADE

It was a smart move to call themselves the Angry Brigade. Lots of people with something to be angry about wondered if they might have something in common. Before that - under the name of the Revolutionary Solidarity Movement - nobody took any notice. But this wasn't righteous anger. It was anarchy on a grand scale - amassing bombs and machine guns to destroy anything that came to mind. They were as indiscriminate as that. They chose as their first target - said the Old Bailey prosecution - the American Embassy in London.

At 11.40pm on the night of August 20, 1967, a white Ford Cortina slid to a halt outside the Grosvenor Square building. A rear window was wound down and a Beretta sub-machine gun blasted away at the embassy. A letter was left on the scene and Communique Number One sent to 'The Times' announcing THEY - the great new protesters who knew better than any of us - had arrived.

For three years they grabbed the headlines with one outrage after another. The police seemed helpless. But then one night in Cell C334 of Brixton Prison - the lid was blown off the cover of anonymity. That was the night Big Jake talked too much. Ironically, it was a moment of unplanned anger that brought careless words from Big Jake - Jack Leonard Prescott, 26 year old overlord of the bomb-happy destructionists.

He was then held on a drugs charge. His link with the faceless men and women of the bombs brigade was not known. Not even suspected. Hateful of authority of any kind and irritated in particular by the lofty manner of one warder, he told a cell crony: "I have some friends who could put a bomb under him."

Once his tongue had thus been loosened, there was no end to the bragging of this Scots-born orphan about the bomb outrages he and others had planned and carried out. In a week's ceaseless chatter and torrent of boasts, he poured out to two cell mates the inner-most secrets of the Angry Brigade.

HOW it planned its attacks in military-style precision and using home-made bombs, the composition of which he illustrated with detailed drawings. And WHO were its victims and WHY it existed. Every word was passed back to the authorities. "This was the break we needed in our hunt for the bombers," a senior Scotland Yard detective admitted last night. "He even trotted out the names of other top fanatics in the movement."

It was a stroke of genius on their part to have him freed on bail. The hunch that he would soon drift back to his old revolutionary haunts paid off. He was shadowed as assiduously as any spy. Closer, in fact, than some have been in the past. Detectives tailed him day and night round squalid Angry Brigade communes in Notting Hill, Islington, Stoke Newington, Colchester, Manchester and Liverpool.

REVEALED at long last - in a dingy first floor flat in Amhurst Road, Stoke Newington - was their arsenal of weapons. Machine guns, pistols, thousands of

117

rounds of ammunition, bomb-making devices, and a John Bull kiddies' printing kit for their communiques. Plus a list of intended VIP victims, Cabinet Ministers, Old Bailey judges, the Attorney General, the Police Commissioner, industrialists, top firms, embassies, consulates, and public buildings including the Post Office Tower. Training manuals, war literature, theses of hate and how-to-destruct, were found around the flat in which the militants made permissive love together while planning their vengeance on society.

WHO and WHAT was the Angry Brigade? They claimed to speak for the ordinary man or woman in the street. But that was not true. They were a tiny minority, with nothing constructive to offer to replace the trail of rubble left behind by their home-made bombs. They claimed: 'We destroy property not people.' But this was a blatant lie. For Home Secretary Robert Carr and his family were lucky to escape unharmed when two bombs demolished part of their Barnet home. And a fire bomb planted on a Spanish plane must have endangered many lives.

They were branded 'Public Enemy No. 1' by the then Home Secretary, Mr. Reginald Maudling. They claimed to have counterparts the world over. Brothers and sisters responsible for angry rioting in Paris, Tokyo and Germany. They opposed the Common Market and claimed responsibility for a series of bomb attacks on British property when Prime Minister Edward Heath visited Paris. They 'supported the workers' but shrank from any kind of work themselves. Their Utopia was a Manson-style hippy commune.

They attracted so-called Women's Libbers to their cause. But the girls not only burned their bras - they learned how to make and plant bombs. The Angry Brigade recruited from the fraternity of rejects of British universities. And others who felt the world owed them a living. Like Big Jake Prescott, now serving 15 years for conspiracy to cause explosions. He had a separate, earlier trial.

Typical of the petticoat Violent Ones was dark-haired, bosomy Anna Mendelson, recruited from the discontents at Essex University, Colchester. The 24 year old daughter of a Stockport councillor was in revolt against everything that the Establishment stood for. Under the bed she shared at Amhurst Road with her lover, 23 year old James Greenfield, was a frightening cache of arms - 33 sticks of gelignite, 11 detonators, two machine guns, a pistol, and ammunition. (So? Stoke Newington's a rough neighbourhood. Ed.)

THE POLICE always topped the list of the Angry Brigade's hate catalogue. They were the Pigs. A target for ridicule and contempt. Prime targets of abuse were Commander Ernest Bond and his right-hand man, Detective Chief Superintendent Roy Habershon - both listed for extermination in the Angry Brigade's Black Diary of enemies. Commander Bond was the Home Secretary's personal choice of a super sleuth to launch the Angry Brigade counter-offensive and track the terrorists down.

But bespectacled, soft-spoken Superintendent Habershon only came into it by *chance. It was just two weeks after he had taken over the 'manor' in which Mr. Carr lives - and on a night he was spending quietly at home at his fireside - that the bombers struck. And from that day on - January 12, 1971 - he never returned to divisional work. He just went on pursuing the angry ones. To get to know their quarry Commander Bond, Superintendent Habershon and others drawn from all divisions, studied most forms of extreme political theory.*

Meanwhile, the bombers were being briefed by their bosses on how to react if arrested. Obstruct and frustrate the Pigs, they were told. An order which some duly tried to obey when eventually detained. And as the relentless hunt went on, the bombers boasted: 'We are getting closer to final victory. We are slowly destroying the long tentacles of the oppressive State machine.' But they were wrong. They had no chance of winning. Not in this country.

That night Granada's 'World In Action' is an Angry Brigade special, during which Anna Mendelson's asked what she thinks the Angry Brigade achieved. She replies;

"Achievement in terms of change, it hasn't achieved anything, anything at all."

Jonathan Raban describes the interview thus in 'Soft City';

Anna Mendelson talked in what is increasingly becoming a characteristic idiom of our time; a style in which familiar words are pronounced as if they were compo-nents of an arcane code. She spoke distractedly in a dream-monotone: phrases like 'working class', 'conspiracy', 'change of consciousness' came out rounded as peb-bles, but what they meant to me was clearly not what they meant to her. When she was asked whether the bombings had had any tangible effect on the progress of the revolution in England, she stared mildly, apparently incomprehendingly at her interviewer and said 'I suppose they must have... yes... they must have, mustn't they...' so vaguely that one felt that one had trespassed illicitly over the far side of her dream.

These intense, private groups, compacted around a core of symbolic objects and ideas are very serious symptoms of a metropolitan condition. They may or may not be politically important in themselves; and when they take a religious turn they may indicate nothing about the spiritual awakening which fond members of the clerisy enjoy forecasting. But the club, the clique, the cell, the commune, the code are proliferating forms in the city. Huddled, defensive, profoundly complacent in their indifference or hostility to the rest of the city, they are the foxholes for all those whom the city has isolated, for whom no larger reality is habitable... In our city, it is easy to drift into a privacy of symbols, a domain of subjective illusions made concrete by the fact that 2 or 3 people have gathered together to conspire in them.'

119

GERONIMO CELL

1972-76: SOONER OR LATER YOU'LL HEAR FROM US AGAIN - THE £1 MILLION LIE - IN STORE FOR MORE TERROR - FINAL COUNT - AFTERMATH - YOU CAN'T ALWAYS GET WHAT YOU WANT - MPLA - UDA - IRA

DECEMBER 14: 'Happy Christmas (War is Over)' by John Lennon is released and another Angry Brigade article appears in 'It' #144, accompanied by the final postscript 'Geronimo Cell' communique;

THE £1,000,000 LIE (by Seymour Wilbur 111)

The nightmare, as Anna Mendelson called it, 6 months of near silence in the bourgeois press, and then an orgasmic splurge on the 'sociological' implications of the Angry Brigade. 'The Sun' did its gory best, but none of the others were far behind. The day after the sentences were announced 600 people marched to Holloway in solidarity with Anna Mendelson and Hilary Creek. When they got there and proclaimed their solidarity hundreds of prisoners answered from windows. When Chris and John arrived at Wormwood Scrubs, the men on their landing were out of their cells, greeting the two with rousing cheers, one prisoner giving John a sweater. They have got the message, they have all had their 'Angry Brigade Trials', every prisoner in a British jail knows all about 'British Justice'.

And of course no one likes to refer to the craziness of it all. Even on the simplest level; Stuart Christie is innocent, therefore he did not have detonators in the boot of his car when he was arrested, therefore the police were lying when they said that he did have the detonators in his possession. John Barker, Hilary Creek, Anna Mendelson, James Greenfield, were found guilty, therefore they did have arms in their flat in Amhurst Road, and the police were not lying. Which lies do you prefer, a big lie or a small one? The police are already convicted by imputation of perjury in the case against Ian Purdie, and now again. 'Oh well they'll be out in 10 years.' Who believes that 10 years in prison is a short time, not anyone who's already spent 18 months as a category 'A' prisoner in Brixton. As Stuart Christie said on the day he was released, "I'd sooner be in a Spanish jail than an English one."

IN STORE FOR MORE TERROR...

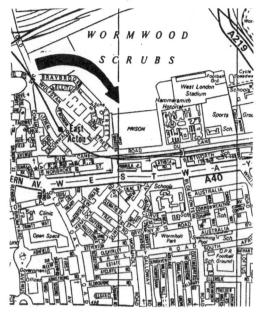

The establishment is already kicking itself on allowing the defence to get a reasonably representative jury, that could understand something about what the defence was trying to put across. 'Justice' James has made it clear that never again will the defence be allowed to cross-examine prospective jurors about their bias. 'What! No Tories allowed on the jury? We can't have that, the police said they were guilty didn't they? Jack Lynch, now, he has the right idea about courts, scrap the jury system, and make a senior policeman's word law. A senior policeman mind you, someone about Habershon's rank would do.'

The police are shifting their position. The moment the trial is ended we hear a strange new sound that 'we haven't caught all the Angry Brigade' and Bond whips out a couple more names from his suspect book. That, he hopes, will account for the fact that whoever the Angry Brigade are, they continued doing whatever they were doing throughout the trial, the prosecution did not have much of a convincing explanation of the Bryant explosion for example. Bond grave-facedly tells the press that we may be in store for 'more terror' and that we will have the 'bomb squad' with us for a long time yet. Bond announced that he is looking for Sarah Poulikakou and Jerry Osner and proceeded to ramble on about letter bombs. The intention is clear: to hound people down, to ram through the convictions, we need hysteria: letter bombs now, that's always good for a bit of public frenzy. Interestingly enough none of the Fleet Street press, who coyly informed us that they had received 'what purports to be an Angry Brigade communique', bothered to quote the excerpt in which letter bombing is condemned.

And here it is: Angry Brigade Communique No. 14; Geronimo Cell. 'Sooner or later you will hear from us again...'

121

It's been a long time brothers and sisters... long angry silence since the sounds of our last explosion, since we attacked the Bryant empire in Birmingham, since angry building workers downed tools in the Woodgate Valley Estate, a long time since Angry Brigade headlines exploded in your breakfast bowl.

Friends, there are so many reasons why... But we are still alive and well. After attacks on Robert Carr, blowing Special Branch HQ at Tintagel House, and spotlighting #1 Fords oppressor, the Batty job... it's time to weigh the balance between revolutionary advances and the gain that repression has ******** ** ****(?). 12 people have been rounded up. No revolutionary group can carry on regardless. We are not military generals or a ruthless elite. If the more the Angry Brigade bombs, the more innocent people are framed, then revolutionary solidarity demands second thoughts and differ-ent actions. THE WORKING CLASS HAS MANY WEAPONS MORE POWERFUL THAN BOMBS. By halting the bombing we threaten something worse. Our worse will always be aimed where it hurts the bosses most, their precious property.

We have shaken the bosses and scared cabinet ministers. We have given them a small dose of their own medicine, a little taste of their own violence. But now is the time to silence capitalist cynics and revolutionary fools. The present spate of letter bombs has absolutely nothing to do with the Peoples' movement, or any cells of the brigade. Letter bombs are a desperate tactic, the product of frustration and impatience. We condemn those who use bombs against civilians, fanatics who care little for human life. Zionism will not be destroyed by killing a few businessmen. We feel for the Arab movement, we support their aims to liberate the Middle East, but the present campaign is indiscriminate and unproductive.

Again, we totally support the liberation struggle of the Irish people. But do not believe that the Provisional IRA are its best supporters. THOSE WHO BOMB WORKERS BOMB THEIR OWN ARMY. Irish nationalism is not enough to defeat the British army. 500 years of imperialism can only be smashed by uniting the class violence, North and South, against the Stormont and Dublin regimes. Connelly's Irish Workers Republic will not be achieved by playing into the hands of the SAS assassination squads. This communique is addressed to all our comrades in Ireland... the Angry Brigade suggests that the Irish people make it clear to the Provisionals that, apart from our class enemies LIFE IS NOT EXPENDABLE. Random terror is the rule of law and order. In the name of socialism, we deny any connec-tion with those who commit inhuman acts. 'Only fascists and government agents attack the public.' (communique 5)

ALL ANGRY BRIGADE ATTACKS HAVE AND WILL BE DIRECT-

ED AT RULING CLASS PROPERTY. REMEMBER WHAT WE SAID IN COMMUNIQUE 5, 'WE ARE NOT MERCENARIES, WE ATTACK PROPERTY NOT PEOPLE, CARR, RAWLINSON, WALDRON WOULD ALL BE DEAD IF WE HAD WISHED.' BUT WE LET THEM LIVE. WE HAVE NO WISH TO MAKE MARTYRS OUT OF RULING CLASS PIGS.

Scratching the Carrs of this world is not our chief concern, but rather protecting the lives of innocent people who are exploited by these bastards. We have always given warnings. We have always used small amounts of explosives. One woman got slightly cut when she refused to accept our warning. This is partly why we have broken our silence. The capitalist cynics are expert at lumping all violence together, except of course their wars that just happen to wipe out millions, and the daily exploitation and degradation of a soul-grinding production line. Our offensive against the ruling class will continue in many different ways, including bombings if they are necessary to demonstrate the morally correct use of political violence. If this communique is hushed up like the Bryant one, and actions we have carried out since then, we shall have to think again about future activities.

Too many people think of the Angry Brigade as just bombers, acting out the undeclared phantasies of millions to blow their bosses up, all harmlessly channelled, rivetted to a single explosive moment. BUT WE DO NOT LIVE THROUGH BOMBS. WE CANNOT BREATHE THROUGH OUR DETONATORS. WE DO NOT CALL OUR LIFE STYLE TNT. Do you think, capitalist fools, that the AB only lives in the shadow of its own acts of destruction? That like moths we wake at dusk in order to fly off upon another moonlight mission?

Brothers and sisters, we have Old Bailey nightmares... the cruel irony of those planted at Amhurst Road, the Stoke Newington 8. The Angry Brigade trial is a trial in the absence of the Angry Brigade. Habershon's gang has been hunting for nearly 2 years. The nearest they ever got was to frame-up known militants like Purdie and Prescott. It is the same desperate logic that hanged Hanratty. They haven't caught us and they can't. That's why friends and sympathisers we've barely rubbed shoulders with have been fitted up. We are not there to defend ourselves for the simple reason that no one we know leaves gelly and detonators in their lounge. Maigret is more real than Scotland Yard fables. We know the truth, the pigs know the truth... the Stoke Newington 8 are innocent. Sooner or later they will be freed. Sooner or later you will hear from us again. The Thalidomide butchers and the lead poisoners will never appear at the Old Bailey. Master criminal Rawlinson aids and abets the covering up of these crimes. The millionaires who pollute our lives have taken out a life long insurance policy called police protection. Every criminal trial ignores the real criminals.

JAIL THE MAUDLINGS, THE CARRS & THE DISTILLERS DIREC-
TORS, GOOD LUCK TO THE STOKE NEWINGTON 8, LOVE, SOLIDAR-
ITY, REVOLUTION. copy this out - destroy the original. COMMUNIQUE
14. ANGRY BRIGADE. GERONIMO CELL.

THE FINAL COUNT: Of the 12 people Habershon set out to arrest and charge
with conspiracy to cause explosions; 5 are convicted and imprisoned, 5 are acquitted and 2 have the charges withdrawn before they come to trial. In 'Underground',
Nigel Fountain summarises the state of the UK scene after the Stoke Newington 8
trial;

*So, amongst Marxists, squatters, claimants, freaks, followers of the Bhagwan, the
Guru Maharaj Ji, rock fans, feminists, Situationist theorists et al, where was there
room left for an underground?*

MARCH 8, 1973: IRA car bomb attacks outside the Old Bailey and Whitehall
leave 200 injured. While 5 tons of Libyan arms destined for the IRA is seized by
the Irish Navy off County Waterford.
JULY: The case of the Stoke Newington 4 goes to the Appeal Court, where the
sentences are duly upheld by Lord Justice Widgery. Though Jake Prescott's is
reduced to 10 the same as the others. A few days later the Gordon Carr Angry
Brigade documentary goes out on BBC and is described by Peter Fiddick in 'The
Guardian', as *'the best piece of factual reporting on the subject we have yet seen
or heard.'* (Gordon Carr is also responsible for documentaries about Michael X
and the Kray Twins.) Close on its tails comes the curious partly fictionalised 'documentary novel' also entitled 'The Angry Brigade' by Alan Burns, published by
Quartet and Allison & Busby. ('The AB' by AB published by A&B. Hmmm?)
And basically it's not very good.

For the record, Habershon makes Commander in 1973 and gets seconded to the
Home Office Research and Planning Office. Commander Bond is promoted to
Deputy Assistant Commissioner at Scotland Yard, before retiring to write his
memoirs. Justice James is appointed Lord Justice of Appeal and Robert Carr goes
on to become Home Secretary.

AUGUST: Hawkwind release 'Urban Guerrilla' single.
AUGUST 18: The idea of urban guerrilla warfare in mainland Britain catches on
when the IRA launch a fire and letter bomb campaign, to disrupt the Old Bailey
bombers trial. One person is killed and up to 400 injured.
DECEMBER 18: IRA Xmas parcel/car bombing campaign in London in reprisal
for jailing of Old Bailey bombers leaves 70 injured. Carlos is also in town,

THE ANGRY BRIGADE

attempting to assassinate Marks & Spencer boss Edward Sieff and setting up PFLP safehouses on Chesterton and Hereford Road in Notting Hill.
DECEMBER 20: ETA assassinate Franco's PM Luis Carrero Blanco with a mine that blows his car over a church.
JANUARY 24, 1974: Carlos bomb attack on Israeli Hapoalim bank in London injures one woman.
FEBRUARY 3: IRA suitcase bomb hidden in luggage compartment of coach on the M62 kills 9 squaddies plus a woman and her 2 children.

But in the end it's not the MPLA, UDA, IRA, ETA, Angry Brigade or Carlos, who finally topple the Heath government but a series of strikes culminating in the Miners' Strike and 3 Day Week of winter 73/74.

MAY 17: 6 SLA/suspected Patty Hearst kidnappers die in gun battle with LAPD.
JULY 17: IRA bomb attack on the Tower of London kills one woman and injures 41 children.
SEPTEMBER 15: Carlos kills 2 and wounds 34 others when he throws a hand-grenade into Le Drugstore in St. Germain des Prés.
OCTOBER 5: IRA pub bombings in Guildford and Woolwich leave 7 dead and up to 100 injured. Guinness Book of Records compiler Ross McWhirter is subsequently shot for sponsoring reward scheme for apprehension of those responsible. Commercial and social life in the West End is severely curtailed by IRA activity.
NOVEMBER 21: IRA bomb attacks in Birmingham result in death toll of 21 and 168 injuries.
ALSO IN 1974: Habershon heads the police investigation into the killing of Kevin Gately in Red Lion Square. Not surprisingly the police are absolved of all responsibility.

1975: As Thatcher replaces Heath as Tory leader, Habershon replaces Robert Huntley as head of the Bomb Squad, in time for the IRA Balcombe Street siege. The (fairly) definitive Gordon Carr Angry Brigade book is published by Victor Gollancz. And there's another press outcry when Hilary Creek and Anna Mendelson, who've both become seriously ill inside, are released on parole after less than 5 years. Barker, Greenfield and Prescott do the full 10 years. Christie moves to the remote island of Sanday in the Orkneys, where he continues publishing 'Black Flag' and the likes of 'Towards A Citizen's Militia' through his own Cienfuegos Press.

As for the Angry Brigade, to quote the introduction to the Alan Burns book; 'The true story of the Angry Brigade will never be told until they publish their memoirs... if they ever do.' And by all accounts they're never going to. Unless you count 'The Christie File'. The Alan Burns intro continues with an uncredited press report;

FOCUS ON THE ANGRY BRIGADE

Who then was responsible for the Post Office Tower bombing and those at Carr's home, Bryant's home in Birmingham, the army barracks in Albany Street, Chelsea Bridge early in September, and the ˙ Royal Tank Regiment HQ in Westminster? At least three have been claimed by the Angry Brigade. But it seems as if the bombings are the work of more than one group. In the words of the Special Branch's 'experts on the left'; 'In calling it the Angry Brigade we're chasing a myth because there is no one organisation called the Angry Brigade. There is a theory that the Angry Brigade is a many headed-hydra.' In other words the example set by the bombings of last year has been followed by independent political groups. In London alone there are thought to be three such groups.

Alan Burns goes onto describe two of the London groups as;

A gang of London street kids living virtually as outlaws, squatting in derelict houses; and a small group of intellectuals who combined a 'straight life' with intermittent urban guerrilla activity.

At the time of the interviews which constitute the book (Spring 1973), the two groups are uneasily linked and there's talk of a nationwide Angry network. Indeed Angry Brigade activity continues for some time after the bust and trial, and still has the occasional resurgence to this day. But the police and the authorities have their victory. They manage to lock someone up and do their bit to kill off the underground scene and take the momentum out of 'the Movement'. For the time being at any rate. As an Angry Brigade associate says at the time; "I think in 3 or 4 years time, even longer, people will relate to what they've done and will think about it and think it's important."

1976: As British mercenaries join UNITA forces in Angola fighting the Marxist MPLA and end up being tried as Dogs of War, the UDA assassinate IRA leader Maire Drumm in hospital, and the IRA launch a new bombing campaign, with one at the Ideal Home Exhibition, another in Tavistock Square and one on the tube at Cannon Street. As well as blowing away British Ambassador Christopher Ewart-Biggs with a culvert bomb in Dublin.

From Up Against The Wall Motherfucker flyer. 1968.

'By Any Means Necessary', 'King Mob Echo' 1968.

LEAVING THE 20TH CENTURY

1967-1977: WE'RE LOOKING FOR PEOPLE WHO LIKE TO DRAW - KING MOB - BLACK MASK - LAMF - SUBURBAN PRESS - THE END OF MUSIC - NEW YORK DOLLS - SEX PISTOLS AND PUNK ROCK

'We contemplate other people destroying the environment we want to destroy.'
(John Barker, talking about the Who, Birmingham 'Radical Arts' mag, 1969.)

Around the same time as the Angry Brigade there's a less well known but equally influential pro-situ group in Notting Hill, known as King Mob. Some of whom are actual card-carrying Situationists, for a while at least. King Mob come out of the mid-60s English branch of the Situationist International / 'Heatwave' group, which consists of Tim Clarke, Chris Gray, 'Revolution of Everyday Life' translator Donald Nicholson-Smith and the dope smuggler/underground press stalwart Charlie Radcliffe. All of whom are expelled from the SI in late 1967 for refusing to side with the Parisian politburo against the New York Black Mask / Motherfuckers group, who Debord and co find ideologically unsound in some way. For the record Charlie Radcliffe jumps before he's pushed, after inventing Pop Situationism with a 'Heatwave' article about 'teddy boys', 'ton-up kids' and 'ravers'.

Sid and John in '68

129

Another factor may have been Chris Gray's boasts of a Notting Hill urban guer-rilla army, which according to Fred Vermorel in 'Sex Pistols: The Inside Story', prompts a visit from Guy Debord himself. So the story goes, when Debord turns up at Gray's place on Cambridge Gardens, the best Gray can come up with is to send him round to new recruit Dave Wise on All Saints. There Debord is none too impressed to find Gray's guerrilla army, the brothers Dave and Stuart Wise, swig-ging McEwan's Export and watching 'Match of the Day'. Debord subsequently storms back to Paris and expels the brit sits. Then Gray and the Wise brothers form King Mob, which Vermorel reckons does infact number up to 60 loosely affiliated members at its height.

The name comes from the late 18th Century Gordon rioters who daubed 'His Majesty King Mob' on Newgate Prison after gutting it in June 1780, just before the French Revolution. In Dave Wise's 'The End of Music (Punk, Reggae: A Critique)', the 20th Century version are said to 'laud and practice active nihilism', similarly to the Sex Pistols and as opposed to the Angry Brigade version of the Clash. Instead of openly political causes, King Mob celebrate any delinquent or anti-social activity. The short-lived 'King Mob Echo' lauds the likes of Jack the Ripper, the child killer Mary Bell and John Christie. King Mob are probably responsible for the 'Christie Lives' graffiti that appears opposite 10 Rillington Place. As 'The End of Music' puts it;

Look at the monstrosities produced by bourgeois society. Isn't that sufficient to condemn the golden afternoon of hippy ideology? There was a greater emphasis on such horrific negatives than the revolutionary negative. Socialism or bar-barism? Rosa Luxembourg's stark choice was giggled at - better barbarism. Better to be horrible than a pleasant, altruistic hippy.

King Mob aspire to be 'a street gang with an analysis' like the Black Mask/Up Against the Wall Motherfucker group, but Fred Vermorel describes the Wise Brothers as stocky northern art lecturers. After King Mob and 'End of Music' they go onto produce various pamphlets the best of which is 'Once Upon A Time There Was A Place Called Notting Hill Gate'; but the best thing they ever did still has to be drinking McEwan's Export and watching 'Match of the Day' when Debord came round. If of course they really did it?

In 1968 King Mob's nihilistic plans include dynamiting a waterfall in the Lake District, with accompanying 'Peace in Vietnam' graffiti (which would've been more anti-rural romanticism than anti-war); blowing up Wordsworth's house in Ambleside with accompanying 'Coleridge Lives' slogan; and hanging peacocks in Holland Park with 'Peacocks is Dead' graffiti. 'End of Music' describes the state of mind behind such thinking as;

It was energy itself that was needed, an excess of energy which fostered an apocalyptic fear of the imposed extended passivity; the Big Sleep; the hunkering down under; the steady job. Fear too, that this fate lay around the corner for each individual who wasn't seen to be radiating personal energy. Do something.

One King Mob plan that does come off and probably their finest hour (though it's a rip-off of Black Mask's 'Mill-in at Macy's') comes when a King Mob contingent visit Selfridges during Christmas 1968. With one of them dressed as Santa Claus (probably not Malcolm McLaren; despite his re-enactment in 'Ghosts of Oxford Street') they proceed to give free gifts to children. Until the store calls the police, who arrest Santa and make the children give back their presents;

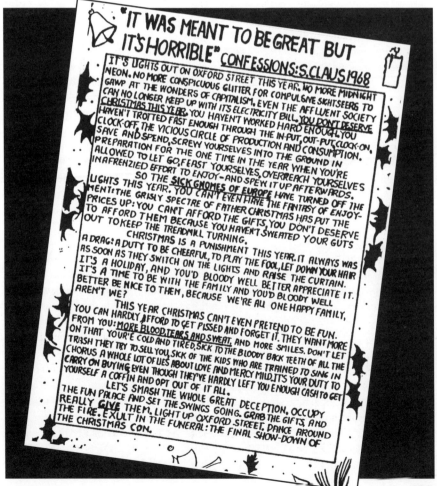

Another King Mob flyer celebrates Valerie Solanas' shooting of Andy Warhol and includes a hit-list of: Yoko Ono, Mick Jagger, Bob Dylan, Mike Kustow, Richard Hamilton, Mario Amaya (also shot by Solanas), David Hockney, Mary Quant, Twiggy, 'it' editor Miles and Marianne Faithfull. They're also responsible for various attacks on art galleries and Wimpy Bars, and for organising a battle between skinheads (who they consider to be 'the working class avant-garde') and greasers in Central London. For the 1969 Notting Hill Carnival King Mob present a 'Miss Notting Hill 69' float featuring a girl with a massive syringe attached to her arm.

'End of Music' goes on to be remarkably sympathetic to the Angry Brigade, describing them as a virtual spin-off of King Mob;

In any case one could always threaten bombs and call for the arming of the working class. The superman/woman militancy and the subsequent terrorism came with the tragic loss of the sense of game and vandalism through theoretical and practical confusion caused by having to confront a fresh series of problems. From the breakdown of King Mob other tendencies developed. One trying to live out the ideologies of a politically conscious hippy life style (akin to the Yippies but more honest) became openly terrorist (the tragedy of the Angry Brigade) while others became careerists in the university set up.

In 1974 Chris Gray falls further from grace with Debord and the American prositus when he publishes 'Leaving the 20th Century (The Incomplete Work Of The Situationist International)'. Gray's translation of texts from the 'Internationale Situationiste' is considered 'a confusionist hodgepodge.' However, another of Chris Gray's ideas comes to a far more fruitful conclusion: 'End of Music' describes how, amongst all the other ideas mooted in '68;

Chris Gray had the idea of creating a totally unpleasant pop group (those first imaginings which were later to fuse into the Sex Pistols) and a spoof, hip, in depth, sociological report of utter degeneration in the sub-cultural milieu to be published by Penguin books and then exposed for the farce it was.

For once this isn't a LAMF idea, though the States do have John Sinclair's White Panthers and their musical wing, the MC5 in 1969. And Mick Farren's White Panthers UK have the Deviants, Pink Fairies, Hawkwind et al. You can still see **'CHRIS GRAY BAND'** graffiti on the way to Victoria Coach station (Or you could anyway, when I first started this). King Mob also claim responsibility for most of the more imaginative West London graffiti, such as the prophetic; **'THE ROAD OF EXCESS LEADS TO THE PALACE OF WILLESDEN'** and **'I DON'T BELIEVE IN NOTHING - I FEEL LIKE THEY OUGHT TO BURN DOWN THE WORLD - JUST LET IT BURN DOWN BABY'**. And:

Proto-Punk King Mob graffiti under the Westway between Ladbroke Grove and Paddington.

As far as anybody knows the anti-music group idea doesn't get beyond the graffiti stage in the hands of Chris Gray. Unless you count the efforts of Charlie Radcliffe's dope smuggling mate, Howard Marks. Described as the Richard Branson of dope by Nigel Fountain in 'Underground', Marks is also partly responsible for the pre-punk record 'Fuck You', which comes out in 1972 on Lucifer Records. An ad for 'Fuck Rock' in 'Frendz' claims;

It's a love song, but the record companies won't touch it, the BBC won't play it, and the shops won't sell it. They think the words are dirty. If you buy it this way we can finish the album.

Not surprisingly the album, entitled 'Big Gun', and the second single 'Prick' both flop and Marks and Radcliffe stick with the dope business. But according to the Howard Marks book 'High Time', the 'Fuck Rock' song writer goes onto work for the Bay City Rollers.

Another LAMF cover of 'King Mob Echo' reads; 'Reich, Geronimo, Dada: Revolutionaries with a message for England', then amongst pistols graphics; 'We're looking for people who like to draw.' According to 'End of Music', Chris Gray continues to use the same hippy entrepreneurism to part rich women from their money, as he forsakes nihilism for mysticism. The anti-Bay City Rollers idea then passes into the hands of two fringe members of King Mob and, '3 or 4 years' after the Angry Brigade bust, Chris Gray's idea becomes a reality in the 'totally

133

unpleasant' form of the Sex Pistols. Debatably an amalgam of Situationist theory and unconscious hooliganism, the idea is mostly put into practice by Malcolm McLaren, the 'Situationist Spiv', who like Gray before him, is assisted by the détourning/plagiarising genius of Jamie Reid. Along with a pro-situ team consisting of; Clash manager Bernie Rhodes, Sophie Richmond from Solidarity/Suburban Press, Roadent, Julien Temple, John 'Boogie' Tiberi, Fred Vermorel from 'International Vandalism', Helen Wellington-Lloyd and of course Vivienne Westwood.

McLaren and Reid graduate to King Mob from Croydon Art College, where as well as designing 'Leaving the 20th Century', Reid is co-founder and designer of the pro-situ 'Suburban Press' (1970-75). McLaren is remembered by Gray as 'a wide-eyed art student', though he soon dumps art for the rag trade and normally only dabbles in politics; helping in the occupation of Goldsmith's College of Art Union, distributing student union cards and heckling James Baldwin as 'the black man's Billy Graham'; before turning to rock'n'roll and dressing the New York Dolls up in red patent leather and hammer and sickle flags. That one doesn't quite come off but in the long hot summer of '76 Punk Rock happens, coinciding with rioting at Notting Hill Carnival and spanning the period of the Baader/Meinhof trial in West Germany.

The Sex Pistols' Situationist influence doesn't come to the fore until after the demise of the actual band. Nonetheless it's there all the way through, similarly to the Angry Brigade. McLaren steps up his habitual use of Situationist imagery in the mid-70s, during the transition of 430 Kings Road from 'Too Fast to Live Too Young to Die' to 'SEX'. Mostly in the form of Alex Trocchi/Valerie Solanas quotes. There's also Club Tabou Lettrist pictures, May '68 slogans and Durruti Column references on 'SEX' shirts and the shop walls. McLaren and Reid bang on about leaving the 20th Century and creating/manipulating situations, while Westwood goes on about urban guerrilla chic, and the Angry Brigade get a namecheck in the 'Anarchy in the UK' fanzine. Then when 'SEX' becomes 'Seditionaries' in 1977 it has a post-modern Biba's 'bomb hole' in the ceiling. As Jon Savage puts it in 'England's Dreaming';

Surrounded by the same Situationist rhetoric that had led Detective Inspector Habershon to the Angry Brigade, the Sex Pistols seemed, for a moment, to be urban guerrillas themselves; unpredictable, deeply destructive, everywhere.

SEX/Seditionaries shop assistant Jordan even tells Vermillion of 'Search & Destroy' that 'Anarchy In The UK'; "was written by an ex-Angry Brigade guy." Jamie Reid (who Jordan probably means) proceeds to détourne Cecil Beaton's picture of the Queen for 'God Save the Queen' and re-uses the 'Boredom buses' from the US pro-situ 'Point Blank' pamphlet for 'Pretty Vacant'. Before firmly cementing the Pop Situationist/Punk connection with the final single 'Holidays in the Sun', in late 1977. This time Reid détournes a Belgian holiday brochure cartoon for the cover. And after subsequent legal action replaces it with the holiday beach picture and 'Nice Drawing' from 'Leaving the 20th Century', along with 'Keep Warm This Winter Make Trouble' from Suburban Press. As Fred Vermorel tells Richard North of 'Zigzag' in 1986;

"The whole Pistols thing was basically a Marxist conspiracy, which sounds ridiculous but that's what it was. You had Jamie Reid, Sophie Richmond and Malcolm sitting around talking radical politics, about how to radicalise this and that, how far can we go with this and that."

But whether the Sex Pistols and Punk Rock actually count as a revolution or a Situationist intervention is open to debate. And there's been quite enough of that already. So suffice to say the punks probably unwittingly recuperate the bits of Situationist theory that filter down to them, and leave themselves wide open to their own recuperation by Thatcher and the yuppies. However the unconscious hooliganism side of it was not to be missed!

'It is the same consoling message that the Situationists and the Hare Krishna people preach: believe it, and the city, with all its paradoxes, puzzles, and violent inequities, will float away before your eyes, a chimera to delude only the hopelessly, cynically earthbound... Notting Hill Gate is a superstitious place because it seems to exceed rational prescriptions and explanations. On the Portobello Road, one feels oneself growing more insubstantial, less and less able to keep a sense of personal proportion in the crowd of people who all look so much poorer, or richer, or wilder, or more conventional than one is oneself. It is certainly hard to keep in touch with one's own self - that diminishing pink blob which rolls and slides like a lost coin in a gutter. The people who float on the tide of metaphysical junk - freaks of all kind - have managed, at a price. The new folk magic of the streets promises to have some unhappy political consequences but as a way of responding to the city it does reflect a truth about the nature of the place which we had better learn to confront.' (Jonathan Raban, 'Soft City' 1974.)

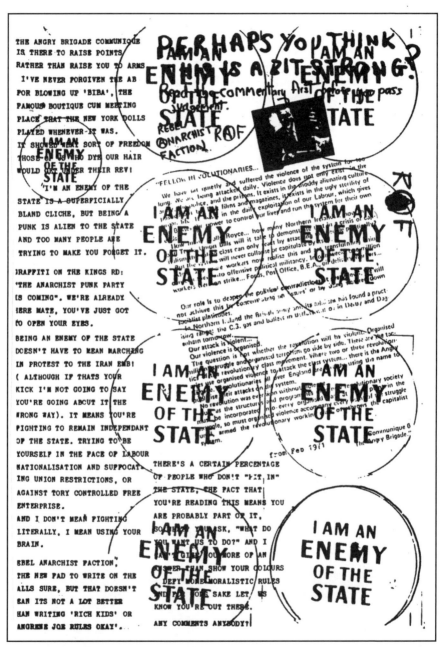

Tony D, 'Ripped & Torn' # 14, October 1978.

WHATEVER HAPPENED TO...

1977 - 1990: IT WAS MEANT TO BE GREAT BUT IT'S HORRIBLE - POST-PUNK - CLASS WAR - IRA - SAS - HIGH TIME - THE 88 DRUG BUST AND THE MOSSAD CONNECTION - NEVER TRUST A HIPPY - OUT OF TIME

As Punk turns into Post-Punk and eventually into Style Culture, various factions emerge. Malcolm McLaren, Jamie Reid and Vivienne Westwood continue to wear their Situationist influences on their record and shirt sleeves, most notably with Bow-wow-wow's 'W.O.R.K.' To a certain extent the Clash and Big Audio Dynamite follow in the Notting Hill Underground tradition, from their 101ers/Elgin Avenue squat scene roots. Clash start out wearing Lettrist style slogan adorned clothes. While the likes of Joy Division/Factory and the Pop Group interpret some of the loftier situ-concepts about urbanism and alienation. Tony Wilson of Factory is probably the most situ-influenced, plagiarising Guy Debord's Lettrist sandpaper book cover for 'Memoires' for the second or third 'Return of the Durruti Column' album cover and literally carrying out the Situ motto 'The Hacienda must be built'. But just about everybody that comes after the Sex Pistols has some sort of cartoon Pop Situationist influence/input. And despite the efforts of RAR/ANL/CND/SWP/NF/BM/BNP Punk and Post-Punk remain largely apolitical with the occasional nod to Pop Situationism (New Order, Frankie Goes To Hollywood, Sigue-Sigue-Sputnik, Pet Shop Boys, KLF). Then there's the likes of Nick Brandt, Mark Downham, Lucy Forsyth and Michel Prigent who return Situationism to its original and probably rightful obscure cult status in the UK with various pamphlets. To a somewhat lesser extent the 'Persons Unknown' bust and trial in 1978 mirrors the Angries. And not forgetting Larry Law's 'Spectacular Times' and Crass, who attempt their own literal translation of 'Anarchy in the UK'. And out of that eventually comes Class War...

137

1979: As Thatch comes to power the IRA assassinate war hero tory Airey Neave, Lord Mountbatten and 18 squaddies at Warrenpoint.

APRIL 30 - MAY 5, 1980: 5 Iraqi backed Arabistan Iranians killed by SAS and 2 hostages by the Iranian separatists in the Princes Gate Iranian Embassy siege.

OCTOBER: IRA H-Block hunger strike for political status. Thatcher/Haughey meeting in Dublin doesn't help British/Irish relations.

MARCH 1981: Bobby Sands and 9 other IRA/INLA prisoners die on hunger strike in Long Kesh. Followed by the Brixton riots.

MAY 9: IRA bomb attack on North Sea oil terminal during Queen visit.

JUNE 13: Blanks fired at Queen on way to Trooping the Colour by 17 year old.

OCTOBER 17: New IRA bombing campaign commences with a nail bomb attack on Irish Guards bus leaving Tower of London, which kills 2 and injures 35. The following week Royal Marine Commandant-General Sir Stuart Pringle loses a leg in IRA car bomb attack. The week after that bomb disposal expert Kenneth Howarth is killed by a booby-trapped bomb in Oxford Street Wimpy Bar.

NOVEMBER: Attorney General Sir Michael Havers escapes unscathed from a bomb attack on his Wimbledon home. Not so Ulster Unionist MP Robert Bradford who's offed outside Belfast University.

COMMUNIQUE: THE BRIGADE IS GETTING ANGRY - AGAIN!

ALMOST TEN YEARS have passed since the political situation in the UK called for the type of direct action as practised by the Angry Brigade. The wheel has turned full circle and we are obliged, once again, to prepare to defend ourselves against the provocations of a virulently anti-working class State and its multi-national manipulators, such as the Steering Committee of the Bilderberg Group and the Trilateral Commission.

SINCE THE THATCHER GOVERNMENT came to power, we have seen a rapid increase in the power of the repressive organs of the State, with a correspondingly obsessive and paranoid emphasis on perfecting its machinery for 'counter-subversion' and 'law and order', political euphemisms for the control and elimination of all real, potential, and imaginary dissidents. The increased expenditure on police, prisons and army, the constant surveillance of trade unionists, harassment of investigative journalists, whistleblowers, environmental, ecological and community activists, the extended deployment of the SAS in Northern Ireland with their assassinations of outspoken socialists such as Miriam Daly and probably Noel Little and Ronnie Bunting, the overt terrorising and intimidation of anyone remotely connected with the struggle in Northern Ireland, the emphasis on population control in police training and the increased number of armed police patrolling the streets of Britain, the new picket laws, etc; all these things indicate that the consensus in British politics is rapidly becoming a thing of the past.

THE ANGRY BRIGADE

THE GROWTH IN STATE SECURITY is necessitated by the political and economic policies of the Thatcher government and its supporters. They know only too well that the economic situation is unlikely to improve without a reversal of their policies. This, in turn, is going to lead to large scale social unrest. There are no workable economic remedies available to them within the monetarist ideology with which they are obsessed. Unemployment will rise steeply, inflation will worsen, more factories and businesses will close down or go bankrupt, apathy and tension will pervade social relationships, the trade union leadership will be unable to restrain the rank-and-file, people will get angrier and more frustrated, and stronger and more desperate forms of control will have to be imposed as the system starts to fail, go hopelessly out of control, and finally collapse altogether.

WHY NOW AND NOT BEFORE? The late sixties and seventies saw a similar period of strident anti-working class hysteria and legislation which led up to the infamous and unsuccessful attempt to control organised labour through the Industrial Relations Bill. This led to the downfall of the Heath government. Having failed to break the labour movement through the courts, the Tories have now turned to a more oblique approach: a deliberate policy of mass unemployment! No doubt the Thatcher clique will be strengthened in their resolve with the election of Reagan, and begin to intensify their policies with each concession made to them.

WE ARE NO VANGUARD, nor do we claim to lead or represent anyone other than ourselves in our resistance to the arrogance of the present government and the misery, frustration and despair created by its selfish and inhuman policies. It is simply that we as individuals are approaching the limits of our tolerance. We see ourselves as an expression of the anger, resistance and hope created by the impending failure of this rapidly polarising society.

IN THE PAST 10 YEARS we have operated mainly in France, Italy, Spain, Germany and North America, and have acquired new skills, expertise, personnel and access to information sources. The more recent actions of Action Directe indicate the strategy and tactics we should employ. As before, there will be no 'mindless terror', no deaths, no hijackings, no hostage-taking of innocent bystanders. We have nothing in common with the tactics or policies of the RAF, Red Brigades, PLO or any other authoritarian group committed to a struggle for power or control of the State at the expense of the man and woman in the street. The social revolution will not be built on the corpses of the old rulers or their functionaries; it can only be built by people taking control of their own lives, asserting their independence, their rejection of the State, of power politics, of authoritarian lifestyles and the competitive values of consumerism forced on us from birth to death. In fighting these evils we also have positive aspirations. We wish for a self-managed society as the only possible basis on which we can build a more just, equitable and libertarian world for ourselves and our children. The increased power of the State, the aggressive confrontation policies of the Thatcher government, the breakdown

139

of a free collective bargaining and consensus in everyday life, the ever increasing estrangement of people from the decision-making process, etc, indicate only one course of action. We must reject and resist this inexorable erosion of our humanity and hopes with whatever means are available to us. WE KNOW WHAT WE ARE GOING TO DO ABOUT IT - DO YOU? THE ANGRY BRIGADE II (IRSM)

1982: On his release from prison John Barker goes to sign on in Swansea. There, according to Class War legend, he's asked what he's been doing recently, to which Barker casually replies, "10 years for blowing up the Home Secretary."
JULY 20: IRA bomb attacks on Household Cavalry in Hyde Park and the band of the Greenjackets in Regent's Park leave 11 people and a number of horses dead.
1983: Communique sent to the Conservative Party;

GETTING ANGRIER! WE PLANTED the small bombs in your northern headquarters at Manchester and Leeds as a reminder to you of the active resistance which exists in this country. We have had enough of you ruining our lives. You commit the worst forms of violence in our society and you don't care. We are thrown out of work, abused by the DHSS and the police, deported and exploited - and still it's not enough for you. Every day we are subjected to greater repression; police powers are increased, more racist laws introduced, 20 years of gains by women are eroded in three, the organised labour movement is under attack, and now we see a policy of summary execution. You think you can crush us, but you're wrong. We will not remain silent in the face of this onslaught - we are fighting back. So far our actions have been aimed at property and not people, but our patience is wearing thin. WE ARE GETTING CLOSER. ANGRY BRIGADES RESISTANCE MOVEMENT.

FEBRUARY: A 'Black Flag' article reads;

Overcrowding in the prisons, general repression and the murder of Barry Prosser earlier this year by screws in Winson Green Prison are some of the reasons given by a group calling itself the 'Angry Brigade Resistance Movement', for the bomb attack on property belonging to the Prison Officers' Training College in Wakefield... One London-based ATS officer is reported to have said that it was unlikely that the Angry Brigade had reformed... it is not possible for the Angry Brigade to 're-form'. It wasn't an organisation, nor was it a single grouping - but an expression of the anger and contempt many people up and down the country had for the State and its institutions. In this sense the Angry Brigade is with us all the time (the man or the woman sitting next to you?) - it neither appears or disappears (or re-forms) but is the natural manifestation of revolt when that revolt is directed at the heart of all that causes suffering: the State.

FEBRUARY 9: IRA kidnap the racehorse Shergar from the Aga Khan's stables in Co. Kildare. Negotiations break down and no more is heard of the Derby winner.
AUGUST: Prison officer stabbed to death in mass IRA breakout from the Maze.
DECEMBER 17: IRA car bomb outside Harrods kills 6 and injures 94.
MARCH 14 1984: Ulster Freedom Fighters wound Sinn Fein leader Gerry Adams.
APRIL 17: WPC Yvonne Fletcher (who I went to school with) is shot dead outside the Libyan People's Bureau on St. James's Square by Libyan diplomat (or CIA) shooting at Libyan demonstrators.
SEPTEMBER 29: IRA arms shipment intercepted off County Kerry.
OCTOBER 12: Slaughter at the Grand: The IRA almost wipe out the entire Thatcher Cabinet with a long-delay-action time bomb planted in the Grand Hotel, Brighton. 5 Tories are killed and many more injured, including Norman Tebbit.

Another Angry Brigade communique ushers in a new era of 'Class War';

ANGRY WORDS. We decided to plant the explosives on the electricity pylon north of Maltby in order to damage the pylon, disrupt the Supergrid link from the Midlands to the North East, and to show that the system is vulnerable. We see the State employing here the techniques of repression developed and practised against the people of Ireland. But we too have learnt lessons from the Irish struggle. As we move towards open CLASS WAR, you will not find us unprepared! VICTORY TO THE HIT SQUADS. Teeside, Humberside, join the ANGRY SIDE. ANGRY BRIGADES RESISTANCE MOVEMENT IRSM.

"Isn't this nice? We must have these Angry Brigade reunions more often"

PAGE

WARLORDS RAN £5M DRUG RACKET TO BUY ARMS

Middle East guns-for-drugs deals

Three Israelis and ex-Angry Brigade member are jailed

By Stewart Tendler, Crime Reporter

...ration Cubby, the Cus-
...s investigation which pro-
...ly ended with the jailing
...hree Israelis and a former
...ber of the Angry Brigade,
...ailed evidence that drugs
... have been traded for
...pons to fuel the Lebanese
...flict.

...t the Central Criminal
...rt, Ishack Zachik Ferman,
...f 32, Asher Sivan, aged 31,
...the Ahron Shtrowise, aged
...were jailed for 10 years
... and James Greenfield,
...38, of Streatham High
...d, south-west London,
...given a six-year term for
...orting 1,800kg of can-
...s. The Israelis pleaded not
...ty to an earlier consign-
...t and the charges were left
...the file.

...p to four tons of Lebanese
...nabis worth £10 million
...smuggled into Britain in
...loads concealed in con-
...ers sent from Beirut by
...stian Lebanese smugglers.

...he second load of nearly
...tons was bound by Cus-
...s, prompting Judge Brian
...stick, sentencing the four,
... speak of a "massive
...portation", one of the larg-
...ored in Britain.

...The former urban
...rrilla who pledged to
... find jobs for East
... Africans

...chind it was one of the
...anon's top drug profits
...s who met Israeli smug-
...s on the neutral ground of
...rus and back at home had
...nections which stretched
...oss the religious divide to
...Muslim-controlled coas-
...le fields of the Bekaa
...ley.

...When the Customs investi-
...s moved in to make
...arrests they found not only
...dence of the drug dealing
... an arms list to

be 50 M20B grenade launchers, Picket rocket launchers
with 330 rockets, 50 Browning
machine guns and a Sam 7B
with 25 rounds.

The list was torn from a pad
and the amount of weapons
was written in red alongside
the weapons themselves re-
corded in black ink.

Customs officials suspect
money from the drug trafficking was used to buy arms for
Christian militia allies of the
Israeli smugglers, who first
made their contacts serving in
southern Lebanon in the Israeli army, or the smugglers
could have been planning a
series of manoeuvres to profit
from both arms and cannabis.
The list could have been a
shopping list or a sales list.

The Israelis may have been
given the drugs on approval
and would pay with ar-
maments bought out of the
profits of the cannabis. There
has also been speculation that
the Israelis were linked in
some way with Mossad, the
Israeli intelligence organisation.

Customs officials say they
believe they have caught part
of one of the largest cannabis
smuggling groups operating
from Lebanon and the Israeli
authorities provided the
cooperation.

The arrested Israelis, described by Customs as tough
professionals, have no criminal records. After their arrest
a fourth Israeli, a former
officer said to have been
involved in planning the raid
on a hijacked plane at Entebbe
airport in Uganda, visited
them in prison.

He went to the US where he
tried to recruit helicopter pi-
lots to rescue his countryman
but was caught by the FBI.

Certainly the Israelis had
other powerful contacts ...
When James Greenfield...

6 The drugs-laden freighter was 2ft shorter inside than out 9

from intelligence in 1985 from
the West Country.

The intelligence showed a
large consignment of cannabis
had reached Britain in 1984 in
a container loaded with Ital-
ian-made pine furniture via
Felixstowe.

Investigators checked
Customs' computers and
found Ferman, as named export agent who had imported a
consignment fitting the intelligence in his own name.

The first members of an
eventual team of 20 investigators began surveillance in
January 1986 on Ferman, who
had lived in Britain for some
years. They found he was
meeting Greenfield, identified
as one of the former senior
members of the Angry Bri-
gade, the urban terrorist group
which grew from student unrest in the 1960s to carry out
bomb attacks on British Cabinet ministers' homes.

In 1972 Greenfield, the son
of poor Lancashire parents
and a Cambridge graduate,
was sentenced to 10 years'
imprisonment with three
other members of the Angry
Brigade.

Greenfield was released in
1978 and became a carpenter.
He was later to tell Customs
investigators he abandoned
this for work which ...

by STUART WINTER

A PLOT to smuggle £5 million of drugs into Britain to finance
Beirut's civil war ended yesterday with the jailing of three
Israelis and a former Angry Brigade anarchist.

They planned to sell cannabis to raise arms money for Christian
militia fighting in Lebanon's war-torn capital.

But the plot was foiled by Customs investigators after a seven-month
operation.

Yesterday at the Old Bailey the three Israelis were each jailed for 10 years
after admitting smuggling. Former Angry Brigade member James Greenfield,
jailed in the Seventies for conspiring to cause explosions, was given a six-year
...ecution.

...e plot began whe
...three Israelis we
...ng in Lebanon dur
...he early 1980s.
... soldiers linked t
... Christian militi
...e of the hidde
... valley overlooke
...ields of cannabis
... the Israelis car
...tain where Ishac
...n, 32, began in
... p the drug smug
...became involved
...wo Angry Briga
...n ... 31-year-o
...eld and his rig
...an John Barker

JAMES GREENFIELD

Arms link as drug smugglers jailed

By Stewart Tendler, Crime Reporter

A former leading figure in the
Angry Brigade terrorist group
and three Israelis were yesterday jailed at the Criminal
Court for smuggling nearly
two tons of Lebanese cannabis
into Britain.

The four were captured in a
Customs operation which also
uncovered evidence of links
between international drugs
trafficking and arms deals.
One of the Israelis was
arrested with an arms list of
infantry weapons including
the Russian ...

toms arrested him when he
tried to leave for Paris after
the consignment of cannabis
arrived from Beirut.

The drug was hidden in the
false bulkhead of a container
holding furniture.

Ferman, of West End Lane,
West Hampstead, north London, was sentenced to 10
years' jail alongside Asher
Sivan, aged 31, a television
producer, from Park Road,
Camden, north London, and
Moshe Shtrowise, aged 34,
from the same address.

The three Isra...

Alert 3.

...I received a ti
...went on the ala
...1986 when t
...Israelis, Ash
...l, and Moshe S
...a 34-year-old t
...urity officer, fle
...is to meet a
...r drugs supplie
...ms men who
...ting last Mo
...ealed contain
...ith cannabis r
...eltzstowe.
...switched to
...hingle and g
...r and Londo
...'sella save
...Customs rad
...tried to m...

£4.5 million haul 3

Drug runners had shopping list of IRA ar...

Gareth Parry on the bizarre background to the case in
which four men were gaoled for smuggling cannabis,
and how Customs officers kept on the trail of suspects
who displayed a measure of professional cunning such
as the officers had seldom come across before

URITY sources believe that
three Israeli army reserv-
... and the former Angry Bri-
...member passed through
drug smuggling charges
...involved in a "drug for
... deal intended to provide
...A with surface to air
...iles and other weapons.

...he four began action on
...supplied a vast quantity of
...oper quality Lebanese Gold
...nabis resin, worth some £5
...lion, into Britain.

...nother former Angry Bri-
...e man believed to have been
...volved is still on the run.
...Ishack Zachik Ferman, aged
...as export agent," Asher
...van," and Moshe Ahron
...trowise, aged 34, "motor
...aler," have remained since
...eir arrest since their
... London 10 months ago.
...Customs special investigators
...warned them with an audio-
...tape plan to bring 1,800 kilos
...of cannabis into the country
...cealed Italian furniture, and
...carried out with the authority
...on of the stricken Christian
... Phalangists.
...But James Greenfield, also
...gaoled yesterday, who once
...mailed for bombing

lift the three Israelis by helicopter from Norwich gaol.

The "shopping-list" bears a
similarity to items in the cargo
of arms bound for the IRA
found aboard the Panamanian-
registered freighter Eksund,
which was seized by French
Customs off Brest in November last November. Five Irishmen
have been charged in Paris
with transporting weapons for
terrorist purposes and detained
in France in connection with
that incident.

But HM Customs' Operation
Chubby, which followed information gleaned from an earlier
drugs seizure in a Bristol container (broccoli) may have happened upon an aberration deep
inside the body of Mossad,
which is acknowledged as one
of the world's efficient, secure
and ruthless secret services.

For Ferman and Sivan are
also believed to be renegade
members of Mossad, which is
known more usually to deal
with defectors by means not of
legal imprisonment but of ex-
tra-legal bullets.

And it is understood that the
first information which led to
capture of the drug smugglers
came from within Mossad
itself.

Now the three Israelis accepted summary imprisonment
may never be known: Mossad talks
not ...

CONSPIRATORS: The three Israeli ex-soldiers who received length... prison sentences yesterday: (from left) Ishack Zachik Ferman, Asher
Ahron Shtrowise; and (far right) John Barker, the former Angry Brigade member who evaded arrest and is now believed to be in hiding

SUMMER 1985: Customs officers receive information that a large quantity of cannabis resin was smuggled into Britain at Felixstowe in 1984, in a container loaded with Italian furniture. Computer checks of all UK importers come up with Ishack Zachik Ferman as the man who brought the furniture in. Ferman, an Israeli army reservist given temporary residence in Britain, is put under close surveillance and in due course leads Customs men to Jim Greenfield and John Barker. In turn, Greenfield leads Customs to two more Israelis, Asher Sivan and Moshe Ahron Shtrowise. The five are subsequently put under 24 hour surveillance by a team of 20 Customs officers, in what is to become known as 'Operation Chubby'.

MARCH 1986: Sivan and Shtrowise meet a Lebanese drugs dealer in Cyprus, who's also known to be in touch with Ferman. Shtrowise also goes to Beirut to meet a Christian Phalange leader, and Jim Greenfield visits, England's answer to Beirut, Manchester to hire a warehouse on the Trafford Park industrial estate. While Greenfield's doing this Customs men find a piece of paper sticking out of his car door with 'Pramaglow Ltd' and Greenfield's accommodation address in Kensington on it.

MAY 18: All of the group meet at Jim Greenfield's flat in Streatham.

MAY 22: The freighter MV Calymnos arrives at Felixstowe, from Beirut, via Salerno. During the night Customs officers come across a container that is 2 feet shorter inside than on the outside. The container is cut open with oxyacetelene torches to reveal 1,800 kilos of top quality Lebanese Gold cannabis resin. Then it's re-sealed with bags of sand and rubble in place of the Leb.

JUNE 3: Greenfield gets an uninvolved firm of hauliers to move the container from Felixstowe to Sheffield, where it stays for a week, while a watch is kept to see if anybody's watching it. However Greenfield is spotted keeping an eye on the container at Felixstowe and as it leaves the docks. Barker is seen around Sheffield and Greenfield again at various points along the route, looking out for surveillance and checking on the truck. From Sheffield it's moved onto the Trafford Park warehouse, via Glossop where it picks up a consignment of paint, by another firm of hauliers. Over the next few days Barker, Greenfield and the 3 Israelis are seen together in Manchester, driving regularly changed hire cars. Then Ferman arranges for yet another haulage firm to take the container from Manchester to Brentford. JUNE 10: As the container moves south down the M1, the surveillance team spot a 1,000cc GRS R100 Suzuki following it. During a stop at Toddington Services, the leather-clad rider, who turns out to be Sivan meets Shtrowise in the restaurant. As the lorry approaches London Sivan is seen checking in cars at traffic lights for signs of police/customs. At this stage the Customs team isn't sure whether they've been spotted or not and later say how impressed they were by the smugglers' counter-surveillance techniques.

JUNE 11: After Customs find out that Sivan and Ferman intend to fly to Paris, Sivan is arrested at Heathrow. Ferman manages to get away but is arrested later at home. Jim Greenfield and Shtrowise are arrested the same day at addresses in London, but John Barker gets away to Greece. Customs men later discover a similar container with another false bulkhead and traces of cannabis resin in a warehouse in Battersea rented by Ferman.

JULY: Ferman, Shtrowise and Sivan are moved to a top security prison after the FBI tip off the Home Office about a plan to chopper them out of Norwich jail.

JANUARY 8, 1988: Jim Greenfield, Ferman, Sivan and Shtrowise receive sentences totalling 36 years, 10 each for the Israelis, 6 for Greenfield, for smuggling 1,800 kilos of Lebanese Gold cannabis resin, worth £5 million, into Britain. Ferman, Sivan and Shtrowise remain stum but Greenfield signs a full confession, implicating the three Israelis and putting himself in some considerable jeopardy. Greenfield opts to serve his sentence in solitary confinement and his wife and daughter are moved to a secret address. Headlines such as 'Drug Runners Had Shopping List of IRA Needs' and 'Warlords Ran £5M Drug Racket To Buy Arms', come from a 'shopping list' of arms found in Ferman's briefcase; '50 M20 3 (or 8) grenade launchers, 10 Picket rocket launchers or similar, maximum fighting range 500p metres (300 rockets); five .50 Browning machine guns; SAM 7b.' Which is similar to a shipment of arms bound for the IRA, seized by French Customs from a Panamanian registered freighter off Brittany in November. There's also some speculation in the press of Mossad involvement. 'The Guardian' says Ferman and Sivan are believed to be renegade Mossad operatives and the first lead in the case apparently comes from Mossad. Jim Greenfield is described by his lawyer as, "extremely interested in the welfare of his fellow human beings," and a person who has "served his debt to society for a cause he no longer believes in." John Barker remains at liberty for the time being, on the run in Greece.

JULY 10, 1990: John Barker is arrested trying to get back into Britain on a false passport.

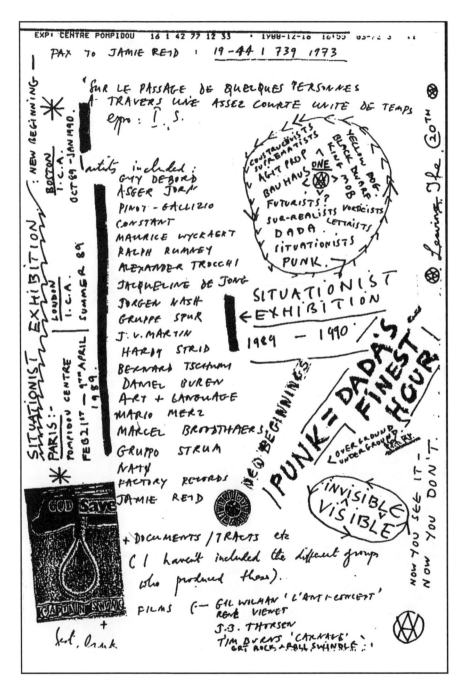

BIBLIOGRAPHY

'AN ENDLESS ADVENTURE... AN ENDLESS PASSION... AN ENDLESS BANQUET: A Situationist Scrapbook'. Edited by Iwona Blazwick. (ICA/Verso. 1989)

'THE ANGRY BRIGADE: A Documentary Novel' by Alan Burns. (Quartet. 1973)

'THE ANGRY BRIGADE: The Cause And The Case' by Gordon Carr. (Gollancz. 1975)

'THE ANGRY BRIGADE 1967-1984: Documents And Chronology'. (Bratach Dubh Documents No. 1. 1978 / Elephant Editions; with introduction by Jean Weir. 1985)

'THE ASSAULT ON CULTURE' by Stewart Home. (Aporia/Unpopular. 1988)

'THE BAADER-MEINHOF GROUP: The Inside Story Of A Phenomenon' by Stefan Aust. (Bodley Head. 1985/7)

'THE BEGINNING OF THE END: France, May 1968' by Angelo Quattrocchi and Tom Nairn. (Panther. 1968)

'BLACK MASK & UP AGAINST THE WALL MOTHERFUCKER: The Incomplete Work Of Ron Hahne, Ben Morea And The Black Mask Group'. (Unpopular/Sabotage. 1993)

'BAMN: BY ANY MEANS NECESSARY: Outlaw Manifestos And Ephemera 1965-70'. Edited by Peter Stansill and David Zane Mairowitz. (Penguin. 1971)

'CAIN'S BOOK' by Alex Trocchi. (Jupiter. 1966)

'CARLOS: PORTRAIT OF A TERRORIST' by Colin Smith. (Sphere. 1976)

'THE CHRISTIE FILE' by Stuart Christie. (Cienfuegos Press, Orkney. 1980)

'COMPENDIUM BOOKSHOP: THE FIRST 25 YEARS 1968 - 1993'. Edited by Chris Render and Phillip Derbyshire. (Compendium. 1993)

'CRANKED UP REALLY HIGH' by Stewart Home. (Codex. 1995)

'THE END OF MUSIC' by Dave and Stuart Wise. (Box V2, Glasgow. 1982)

'ENGLAND'S DREAMING: Sex Pistols And Punk Rock' by Jon Savage. (Faber & Faber. 1991)

'THE ENRAGES AND THE SITUATIONISTS IN THE OCCUPATION MOVEMENT - FRANCE, MAY-JUNE 1968' by Rene Vienet. (Editions Gallimard. 1968)

'FALSE MESSIAH: THE STORY OF MICHAEL X' by Derek Humphry and David Tindall. (Hart-Davis/MacGibbon. 1977)

'FROM MICHAEL DE FREITAS TO MICHAEL X' by Michael Abdul Malik. (Andre Deutsch. 1968)

'HIGH TIME: The Life And Times Of Howard Marks' by David Leigh. (Heinemann/Unwin. 1984)

'HITLER'S CHILDREN' by Jillian Becker. (Michael Joseph. 1977)

'HUNTING MARCO POLO: The Pursuit And Capture Of Howard Marks' by Paul Eddy and Sarah Walden. (Bantam. 1991)

'IF YOU WANT PEACE PREPARE FOR WAR, AND A POLITICAL STATEMENT' by the Stoke Newington 8 Defence Group. (1971-2)

'INVISIBLE INSURRECTION OF A MILLION MINDS: A TROCCHI READER'. Edited by Andrew Murray Scott. (Polygon. 1991)

'IMPRESARIO: MALCOLM MCLAREN AND THE BRITISH NEW WAVE' by Paul Taylor. (New Museum of Contemporary Art/MIT. 1988)

'THE IRA' by Tim Pat Coogan. (Pall Mall/Fontana. 1970)

'LAST GANG IN TOWN: The Story And Myth Of The Clash' by Marcus Gray. (4th Estate. 1995)

'LEAVING THE 20th CENTURY'. Edited by Chris Gray. (Free Fall. 1974)

'LIKE A SUMMER WITH A THOUSAND JULYS' by Nick Brandt. (BM Blob. 1982)

'LIPSTICK TRACES: A Secret History Of The 20th Century' by Greil Marcus. (Secker & Warburg. 1989)

'MR. NICE' by Howard Marks (Secker. 1996)

'ON THE POVERTY OF STUDENT LIFE: Considered In Its Economic, Political, Sexual And Particularly Intellectual Aspects And A Modest Proposal For Its Remedy' by Mustapha Khayati. (Dark Star/Rebel Press/Edition Champ Libre. 1972)

'ON TERRORISM AND THE STATE' by Gianfranco Sanguinetti. (Chronos. 1979)

'ONCE UPON A TIME THERE WAS A PLACE CALLED NOTTING HILL GATE' by Dave and Stuart Wise. (BM Blob. 1988)

'PARIS: MAY 1968' (Solidarity pamphlet #30. 1968)

'PARIS: MAY 1968' (Dark Star/Rebel Press)

'PHANTOM AVANTGARDE' by Roberto Ohrt. (Edition Nautillus. 1990)

'PLAYPOWER' by Richard Neville. (Cape/Paladin. 1970)

'THE POLITICS OF COMMUNITY ACTION: A DECADE OF STRUGGLE IN NOTTING HILL' by Jan O'Malley. (Bertrand Russell Peace Foundation. 1977)

'PROTEST IN PARIS' by Bernard E. Brown. (General Learning. 1968)

'REBEL VIOLENCE VERSUS HIERARCHICAL VIOLENCE: A Chronology Of Anti-Hierarchical Violence In Mainland UK, July 1985 - May 1986.' (BM Blob. 1986)

'THE REVOLUTION OF EVERYDAY LIFE' by Raoul Vaneigem. (Rebel Press. 1983)

'ROCK FILE 1 & 2'. Edited by Charlie Gillett. (New English Library/Panther. 1972/5)

'ROCK LANDMARKS: A To Z Guide To London's Rock Geography' by Marcus Gray. (Omnibus. 1985)

'THE SEX PISTOLS: THE INSIDE STORY' by Fred and Judy Vermorel. (Star Universal. 1978 / Omnibus. 1987)

'THE SITUATIONIST INTERNATIONAL ANTHOLOGY'. Edited by Ken Knabb. (Bureau of Public Secrets. 1981)

'THE SOCIETY OF THE SPECTACLE' by Guy Debord. (Black & Red. 1973)

'SOFT CITY' by Jonathan Raban. (Hamish Hamilton/Collins Harvil. 1974)

'STREETFIGHTING YEARS: AN AUTOBIOGRAPHY OF THE SIXTIES' by Tariq Ali. (Collins. 1987)

'SUBCULTURE: THE MEANING OF STYLE' by Dick Hebdige. (Methuen. 1979)

'TEXTS AND POSTERS FROM THE REVOLUTION' (Atelier Populaire. 1968)

'TO THE ENDS OF THE EARTH: THE HUNT FOR THE JACKAL' by David Yallop. (Jonathan Cape. 1993)

'TOWARDS A CITIZENS MILITIA: Anarchist Alternatives To NATO And The Warsaw Pact'. IRSM/1st of May Group. (Cienfuegos Press. 1980)

'THE TRIALS OF OZ' by Tony Palmer. (Blond & Briggs. 1971)

'UNDERGROUND: The London Alternative Press 1966-74' by Nigel Fountain. (Comedia/Routledge. 1988)

'UP THEY RISE: The Incomplete Works Of Jamie Reid' by Jamie Reid and Jon Savage. (Faber & Faber. 1987)

'THE VERITABLE SPLIT IN THE INTERNATIONAL' by Guy Debord and Gianfranco Sanguinetti. (Chronos. 1974)

'WAR WITHOUT END' by Christopher Dobson and Ronald Payne. (Harrap/Sphere. 1986)

'WATCH OUT KIDS' by Mick Farren and Edward Barker. (Open Gate. 1972)

'THE WICKED WAYS OF MALCOLM MCLAREN' by Craig Bromberg. (Omnibus. 1989)

'YOUNG ADAM' by Alex Trocchi. (NEL. 1966)

Further articles in; 'ANARCHIST REVIEW', 'ANARCHY', 'BLACK DWARF', 'BLACK FLAG', 'BLOCK', 'CATALYST TIMES', 'CITY LIMITS', 'CLASS WAR', 'EVENING NEWS', 'EVENING STANDARD', 'DAILY EXPRESS', 'FACE', 'FRIENDS' / 'FRENDZ', 'GROVE' / 'KENSINGTON SOURCE', 'GUARDIAN', 'HEATWAVE', 'HERE AND NOW', 'I-D', 'INDEPENDENT', 'INK', 'INTERNATIONAL TIMES', 'KENSINGTON NEWS', 'KENSINGTON POST', 'KING MOB ECHO', 'MAIL ON SUNDAY', 'MELODY MAKER', 'DAILY MIRROR', 'MODERN REVIEW', 'MOLE EXPRESS', 'NME', 'OZ', 'PADDINGTON MERCURY', 'POINT BLANK', 'RAPID EYE (MOVEMENT)', 'RED MOLE', 'RIPPED & TORN' / 'KILL YOUR PET PUPPY', 'SEARCH AND DESTROY' / 'RE/SEARCH', 'SEMIOTEXTE', 'SMILE', 'SNIFFIN' GLUE', 'SOLIDARITY', 'SOUNDS', 'SPECTACULAR TIMES', 'THE SUN', 'TELEGRAPH', 'TIME OUT', 'TIMES', 'TODAY', 'TRANSGRESSIONS', 'VARIANT', 'ZG' and 'ZIGZAG'.

televisionaries
the red army
f a c t i o n
story
1963-1993
tom
vague

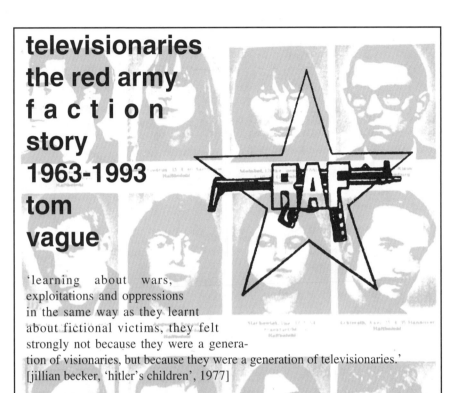

'learning about wars,
exploitations and oppressions
in the same way as they learnt
about fictional victims, they felt
strongly not because they were a genera-
tion of visionaries, but because they were a generation of televisionaries.'
[jillian becker, 'hitler's children', 1977]

'it was all very vague. we talked about vietnam and then we moved onto other things.' [hans-joachim klein - revolutionary cells]

an irreverent chronological history and analysis of the red army faction, as they shoot and bomb their way through the last three decades of western capitalism. from student radicalism to stammheim to euroterrorism, this is the only book in print that charts the rise and fall of the urban guerrilla group that launched a thousand t-shirts. a revised and updated version of the legendary 'televisionaries' issue of vague, includes not only the raf, but june 2nd movement, red brigades, action directe, revolutionary cells, ccc and carlos the jackal, bringing a barbed pop culture view to the most explosive events of the last 30 years. profusely illustrated throughout, with over 30 photographs and cool graphics with guns.

isbn 1 873176 47 3 vague 26 a5 112pp available for £4.50/$6.95 post paid from ak press, po box 12766, edinburgh eh8 9ye, scotland / po box 40682, san francisco, california 94140-0682 usa.

VAGUE 1977-92

a fourteen and a half years' struggle against lies, stupidity and cowardice: a reckoning with the destroyers of the punk rock movement from anarchy in wiltshire to the end of music

through PUNK - POST-PUNK - ANARCHO-PUNK - POSITIVE-PUNK - NEGATIVE-PUNK - INDUSTRIAL -POST-INDUSTRIAL - CYBER-PUNK - CIDER-PUNK - NO-WAVE - NOISE - HARDCORE - HIP-HOP - SITUATIONISM - POST - POST - MODERN PUNK

featuring ADAM AND THE ANTS - THE ANGRY BRIGADE - BOW-WOW-WOW - WILLIAM BURROUGHS - CLASH - CRASS - DECODER - EINSTURZENDE NEUBAUT-EN - ENGLAND'S DREAMING - FALKLANDS DEATH THREATS - GANG OF FOUR - IF.... - JOY DIVISION - KING MOB - LAIBACH - LYDIA LUNCH - CHARLES MANSON - MALCOLM MCLAREN - PARIS '68 - POP GROUP - PSYCHIC TV - RAMONES - JAMIE REID - JON SAVAGE - SEX PISTOLS - SIOUXSIE AND THE BANSHEES - SITUATION-IST INTERNATIONAL - SOUTHERN DEATH CULT - MARK STEWART AND THE MAFFIA - THROBBING GRISTLE - UNEMPLOYMENT - VIZ - X-MAL DEUTSCHLAND

isbn 1 873176 72 4 vague 25 a4 114pp available for £7.95 / $11.95 from ak press, po box 12766 edinburgh eh8 9ye, scotland / po box 40682 , san francisco, ca 94140-0682 .

152

VAGUE 24: THE WEST ELEVEN DAYS OF MY LIFE: Notes from the Portobello Style Underclass/Happy Mondays/Everton/Vague World cartoon/ Red London/Underground/Bugs & Drugs
£3.00 inc p&p (£3.50 overseas)

VAGUE 23: GOD TOLD ME TO DO IT: Performance - Donald Cammell/ Twin Peaks diary/William Gibson and Bruce Sterling/Hype/Vagrunts 2/ Sniffin Ralgex 3/Defiant Pose/Richard Allen
£3.50 inc p&p (£4.00 overseas)

VAGUE 22: MEDIA SICKNESS (MORE CONTAGIOUS THAN AIDS): Margi Clarke/Jamie Reid (cover)/Ralph Rumney/Situationist Exhibition/ England's Dreaming extracts/Cheap Holidays (Berlin /Prague/ Budapest)
£3.50 inc p&p (£4.00 overseas)

VAGUE 21: CYBER-PUNK: England's Dreaming - Jon Savage interview/ London's Outrage/City 68/77/88/2000/Mark Downham/Assault on Culture/Class War by Stewart Home/Bob Black/Jamie Reid
£3.50 inc p&p (£4.00 overseas)

AVAILABLE FROM AK DISTRIBUTION, PO BOX 12766, EDINBURGH EH8 9YE, SCOTLAND.

VAGUE/ROUGHLER

PRESENTS

ANARCHY IN THE UK

BOMB

WITH MUSIC AND POETRY FROM:-

CONTROL DATA   DOLE QUEUE SANTAS
SOUND SYSTEM   HELEN SHADOW
RAY ROUGHLER JONES   MARK JACKSON
TOM VAGUE   DESTRY   AND SPECIAL GUESTS
JOE CAIRO
PAUL STEWART

THURSDAY OCTOBER 27th 1994
7.00pm - 12.30am £3.00

ST. PIUS X COMMUNITY CENTRE
ST. CHARLES SQUARE, OPPOSITE FIRE STATION,
LADBROKE GROVE W10.

154

WILD WEST 11

English Psychogeography

155

'Notting Hill is a rise or high ground of the common earth, on which men have built houses to live in, in which they are born, fall in love, pray, marry and die... These little gardens where we told our loves. These streets where we brought out our dead. Why should they be commonplace? Why should they be absurd? There has never been anything in the world absolutely like Notting Hill. There will never be anything quite like it to the crack of doom... And God loved it as he must surely love anything which is itself and unreplaceable,'

- G.K. Chesterton, 'The Napoleon of Notting Hill', 1904.

'For some the Grove was a testing ground in which they lived wild and free, uninhibited by laws and respectability. This was how it was at the end of the 50s, before the bulk of men could save enough to send for the women and children, who would turn the cowboys into settlers. To be an immigrant anywhere in London meant that, out in the open, you ran a gauntlet of hostility, until you were safely forted up behind locked doors. It was only in Notting Hill that there was a public life. Clubs, restaurants, cafes, music, street corner talk. This was the work of the immigrants, many of them bad boys who set out to make Notting Hill a playground where bad boys could have fun.'

- Mike Phillips, 'Notting Hill in the 60s'

'Ludo did a most marvellous doorstepping job on President Kennedy. And what's more President Kennedy recognised Ludo and said; "Oh, I've just read your book about Notting Hill Gate."'

- Paul Fox, head of BBC Current Affairs on Ludovic Kennedy's meeting with JFK.

'Our sorties into the bilges of the Paddington slums continued. We started going regularly to a little coffee bar on a street where the rubbish was only cleared once a week. Children ran barefoot along the pavements in search of their mothers in pubs. Babies tumbled naked in the squares behind the Grand Union Canal which runs down from Little Venice, through Paddington and out towards the gas works and cemeteries. Paddington had succeeded Soho as the capital of the British Underworld. "I think they're smoking pot somewhere here," Stephen said one evening. "I can smell it." It was a strange musty smell. "I'll see if I can get some," I said. "What do I ask for?" "Grass or weed." I was about to start on a new adventure which eventually led to disaster...'

- Christine Keeler, 'Mandy, Rachman and Me', 'News of the World' 12/10/69.

'Rachman gave his name to the language, but that's about all he ever gave anyone. He could have been several people or merely the front man for others. But he came from nowhere, took on a mythological aura, set forces in train which would alter the district forever, enact laws, and change the course of important social patterns. Then he disappeared, carrying his secrets with him. Existential, don't you think?'

- Mike Phillips, 'Notting Hill in the 60s'.

'At the end of his prison sentence Michael returned to hustling in the Grove. Around this time he developed an interest in those parts of London, such as the Portobello Road, where trendy whites, mostly in their late teens and early 20s, and lucky enough to have allowances from their parents, were setting up avant-garde record stalls and bookshops. Michael was colourful enough to be accepted by a great many of them uncritically and dabbled with them in a few minor business schemes, funded mainly by rich young women...'

- Derek Humphry and David Tindall, 'False Messiah: The Story of Michael X', 1977.

'He bought half a pound or even an ounce of dope at a time from Plinston, and sold it around the streets of Portobello Road, which seethed with bangles and beads and shoulder-bags and patchouli and incense. It was a very long-haired scene...'

- David Leigh, 'High Time: The Life and Times of Howard Marks', 1984.

'In Notting Hill Gate in London, or it might be Greenwich Village in New York, the unreasonable city has come to the point where it cannot be ignored by even the civic authorities. The streets around Ladbroke Grove, with their architecture of white candy stucco, are warrens of eccentric privateness; they are occupied by people who have taken no part in the hypothetical consensus of urban life - the poor, the blacks, the more feckless young living on National Assistance or casual jobs on building sites or bedsitter industries like stringing beads or making candles. The district is notoriously difficult to police: it has a long, 25 year old record of race-riots, drug arrests, vicious disputes between slum landlords and their tenants, complaints about neighbours and petty litigation. Like many impoverished areas in big cities, it is picturesque in the sun, and Americans walk the length of the street market in the Portobello Road snapping it with Kodaks; but on dull days one notices the litter, the scabby paint, the stretches of torn wire netting, and the faint smell of joss-sticks competing with the sickly sweet odour of rising damp and rotting plaster. Where the area shows signs of wealth, it is in the typically urban non-productive entrepreneurism of antique shops and stalls. Various hard-up community action groups have left their marks: a locked shack with FREE SHOP spraygunned on it, and old shoes and sofas piled in heaps around it; a makeshift playground under the arches of the motorway with huge crayon faces drawn on the concrete pillars; slogans in white-wash, from SMASH THE PIGS to KEEP BRITAIN WHITE. The streets are crowded with evident isolates: a pair of nuns in starched habits, a Sikh in a grubby turban, a gang of West Indian youths, all teeth and jawbones, a man in a fedora, greasy Jesus Christs in shiny green suede coats with Red Indian fringes at their hems, limp girls in flaky Moroccan fleeces, macrobiotic devotees with transparent parchment faces, mongrel dogs, bejeaned delivery men, young mothers in cardigans with second-hand prams. These are the urban spacemen, floating alone in capsules of privacy, defying the gravity of the city...'

- Jonathan Raban, 'Soft City', 1974.

'When I think of the punk years, particularly 1977, I always think of one particular spot, just at the point where the elevated Westway diverges from Harrow Road and pursues the line of the Hammersmith/City tube tracks to Westbourne Park station. From the end of 1976, one of the stanchions holding up the Westway was emblazoned with a large graffito which said, simply, 'THE CLASH'. When first sprayed, the graffito laid a psychic boundary marker for the group - this was their manor, this was how they saw London. When it was eventually painted over, in the late 80s, long after the Clash had disappeared, it coincided with the final disappearance of their London. In 1976 and 1977, the Clash had recast the city in half-gleeful, half-tearful songs like 'London's Burning'; 'Up and down the Westway, in and out the lights/What a great traffic system, it's so bright/I can't think of a better way to spend the night/Than speeding around underneath the yellow lights.' By the late 80s, 'London's Burning' was a prime-time LWT serial and the spaces in W11, W10 and W9, which the group had sped through, were being filled in.'

- Jon Savage, 'Punk London', 'Evening Standard', 1991.

ENTRANCE TO HIPP - LONG HAIR - BEATNIKS - DRUGGIES - FREE LOVE - NO BLACKS - NO IRISH - NO DOGS - 10 RILLINGTON PLACE - 81 POWIS SQUARE - CITY OF SPADES - 1958 - WHITE RIOT - CHRISTIE - RACHMAN - MICHAEL X - COLIN MACINNES - CHRISTINE KEELER - J.G. BALLARD - HOWARD MARKS - JOHN BINDON - ABSOLUTE BEGINNERS - PERFORMANCE - MANGROVE - UNDERGROUND PRESS - ANGRY BRIGADE - KING MOB - THE WESTWAY - TRELLICK TOWER - 76 / 77 RIOTS - PUNK - REGGAE - HIP-HOP - LONDON FIELDS KILLS ME - JUNGLE WEST 11 -

VAGUE 28 - TO BE PUBLISHED BEFORE WE LEAVE THE 20TH CENTURY

AK Friends
PRESS of AK Press

In the last 12 months, AK Press has published around 15 new titles. In the next 12 months we should be able to publish roughly the same, including new work by Murray Bookchin, CRASS, Daniel Guerin, Noam Chomsky, Jello Biafra, Stewart Home, new audio work from Noam Chomsky, plus more. However, not only are we financially constrained as to what (and how much) we can publish, we already have a huge backlog of excellent material we would like to publish sooner, rather than later. If we had the money, we could easily publish 30 titles in the coming 12 months.

Projects currently being worked on include previously unpublished early anarchist writings by Victor Serge; more work from Noam Chomsky, Murray Bookchin and Stewart Home; Raoul Vaneigem on the surrealists; a new anthology of computer hacking and hacker culture; a short history of British Fascism; the collected writings of Guy Aldred; a new anthology of cutting edge radical fiction and poetry; new work from Freddie Baer; an updated reprint of *The Floodgates of Anarchy*; the autobiography and political writings of former Black Panther and class war prisoner Lorenzo Kom'boa Ervin, and much, much more. As well as working on the new AK Press Audio series, we are also working to set up a new pamphlet series, both to reprint long neglected classics and to present new material in a cheap, accessible format.

Friends of AK Press is a way in which you can directly help us try to realize many more such projects, much faster. Friends pay a minimum of $15/£10 per month into our AK Press account. All moneys received go directly into our publishing. In return, Friends receive (for the duration of their membership), automatically, as and when they appear, one copy free of every new AK Press title. Secondly, they are also entitled to 10 percent discount on everything featured in the current AK Distribution mail-order catalog (upwards of 3,000 titles), on any and every order. **Friends,** if they wish, can be acknowledged as a **Friend** in all new AK Press titles.

To find out more on how to contribute to Friends of AK Press, and for a Friends order form, please do write to:

AK Press	AK Press
PO Box 40682	P.O. Box 12766
San Francisco, CA	Edinburgh, Scotland
94140-0682	EH8 9YE

AK DISTRIBUTION

...for more information on armed struggles and all your reactive reading...

PO BOX 12766 EDINBURGH EH8 9YE

welcome to the mardi gra experience

lwa communique statement of intent

if you're not busy being born, you're busy dancing to crap house music. all the transvestites in sad yorkshire nightclubs are made to dress the same and have the same make-up, representing the 1970s. in fashion as in everything else, capitalism can only go backwards - they've nowhere to go - they're dead. the future is ours. life is so boring there is nothing to do except spend all your wages on the latest flares or platforms.

leeds brothers and sisters, what are your real desires? dance round your handbags in some naff 70s disco, look sad, empty, boring, drinking evian water? or per-haps blow it up or burn it down. the only thing you can do with provincial discos - called nightclubs - is wreck them. you can't reform 70s fashion and hand-bag house music. just kick it till it breaks. revolution.

shake in your high heels leeds vague the power of the original london punk rock hip-hop vague will soon wipe you out.

by any means necessary. lwa.

vague 27. london. leaving the 20th century.